For Sandra with best wishes

Archie Foley

C000088707

MORE FOOTPRINTS
IN THE SAND

local history from *The Portobello Reporter*

Edited by Archie Foley & Peter E Ross

A L Foley

First published 2020 by A L Foley,
21/1 Joppa Road, Edinburgh, EH15 2HA

Copyright the Editors and Contributors severally 2020.

All rights reserved. No part of this book may be reprinted
or reproduced or utilised in any form or by any electronic,
mechanical or other means, now known or hereafter invented,
including photocopying and recording or in any information
storage or retrieved system without the permission in writing
from the Publisher.

ISBN: 978-0-9934028-2-1

Book design and layout by Peter E Ross

Cover photograph from the Archie Foley Collection,
photograph by Law & Kerr, Portobello,1868.

Fonts used: headers in Cochin originally designed by Georges
Peignot; main text Bodoni 72 designed by Dmitry Kirsanov.

CONTENTS

– ACKNOWLEDGEMENTS –

Thank you to Nicky Bird, Jim Crockett, George Haggarty Sheila Love, Brenda Molony, Margaret Munro, Geoff Pearson, Patricia Ralph, and John Stewart for giving permission for their articles to be included in the book. We are also grateful to Andrew Boyd acting for his late father Sydney Boyd and similarly Noveen Strachan for her late husband Drew Strachan.

We have not been able to contact other named contributors or their representatives and would appreciate any information that would help us to do so.

The Coat of Arms of Portobello Burgh Council featured sailing ships and cannons in its quarters referencing Admiral Vernon's capture of Puerta Bella in Panama from the Spanish in 1739.

– FOREWORD –

When we decided that it would be a nice idea to publish another selection of local history pieces from *The Portobello Reporter* in 2020 to celebrate 40 years of publication everything seemed so straightforward. Like last time we would select and collect the articles, then have regular meetings sharing a computer to put them together, arrange a pre-publication mention and perhaps a review in the June and September issues of the *Reporter*, and get the book printed and published in time to have it in the Portobello Book Festival in October.

Then came Covid-19 followed by lockdown! Close quarter cooperative editing was no longer possible, and the *Reporter* suspended publication after the issue of its Spring edition at the beginning of March. At the time of writing, however, the group is holding virtual meetings to prepare a winter edition.

After some delay there came the cheering news from the organisers of the Book Festival that it would be held on its advertised dates, but online, with original contributors appearing "in a virtual format".

A look back 30 years reveals a period of suspended publication that ended happily. In December 1989, it was announced in the paper that following the retirement of Maureen Child as editor it was "taking a breather" while possible ways forward were investigated. During the breathing spell a new editorial group was formed, and operations moved from Portobello to Joppa. In December 1990, the first edition of its successor was published. Crucially, this would not have been possible without the resumption of financial support provided by advertising placed by local businesses. It was rebranded as *The New Porty Reporter*, but reverted to its original name in 1995.

The paper's founders promised readers that in addition to reporting on local people in the news and current events they would "bring you Portobello's history and reminiscences". This promise has been kept over the past 40 years and the history page(s) are an intrinsic and popular part of the paper. This selection of personal stories and reminiscences, and accounts of events, places and individuals reveal Portobello as a community where people lived and worked not just as a holiday resort.

LOOKING BACK
− MEMORIES FROM 80 YEARS −

Mrs Isa Brown has written in about some fascinating " Portobello Remembered" by her mother. Mrs Euphemia Williamson was born in Ramsay Place on 9th June 1892. She left 6 years ago to live with her daughter in Dalkeith but her interest in Portobello is still strong.

Mrs Williamson was one of thirteen, including two sets of twins. Her father, Samuel McQuillan, was a papermaker in the Portobello paper mill. She and her brother, Willie, now 80 and living in Clermiston, are the only two of the family now alive. When she left school at 14, she went to work in a small pottery in Rosebank Lane, run by a Mr Hay. Her job involved sitting on a brick wall down a hole and turning the wheel for the man who made the flowerpots. A year later, she went to Mitchell's brick works. They made pots as well as bricks, though the wheel was driven by machinery. She worked for a Mr Fraser for 5 years there, and then left to marry Thomas Williamson just after her twentieth birthday, her husband was a bottle-maker at Cooper's works.

Emergency Services Then

In those days there was no fire engine. Instead the fire station in Ramsay Lane had a barrow painted red. Mrs Williamson recalls that one fireman in the shaft pulled, another pushed, and all the 'bairns' helped. Inside the barrow was a hose and an axe. In case of drowning accidents, a stretcher with a cover was ready at the entrance to the old library. For less urgent medical mishaps, Portobello's Dr John Balfour walked to his patients, until he bought a bicycle. Then he used a cab and horse driven by Mr Neilands, a neighbour of Mrs Williamson's. Later he got himself a car. It was said that "his was the ever-open door". Like fire and illness, other unpleasant aspects of life were generally evident, and not hidden away as they are now. Mrs Williamson recalls the mortuary and the slaughterhouse beside each other in Pipe Street.

Play

The first show ground was opened at the foot of Figgate Street by "Evans−the show people". At the foot of Pipe Street, one of the entertainers, Sam Thomson, used to sing:

"Follow me, and I'll lead you in a fearless manner,
and we'll show you what we can do under
the hen-pecked husbands banner!"

Fred Smart had a happier version of family life:
"You are my sister—the only one I've got,I will give you shelter,
though humble be my cot
Though sheltered by a sweetheart who once called you his own,
You'll never want a shelter while your brothers got a home."

Mrs Williamson thinks they spoilt Tower House by building the arcade in front of it. The house belonged to a Mr Gray who kept two lovely lawns down to the Prom. He got the nickname "Pie Gray" because he treated all the children whose fathers were unemployed to a trip to Polton near Bonnyrig. They all had a label tied to their coats and marched to the station Brae for the train. On arrival, they got a pie and milk. Mrs Williamson was one of the children, although she shouldn't have been— her father was em ployed!

Work

At the foot of Pipe Street was a bottle-works called the "Bees Wing". It belonged to Mr Wood who also owned another bottle-works off Baileyfield Road. With access to part of the sands, he could get the sand needed by his other bottle-works. Cooper's bottle-works had to get their sand from France. At the start of the First World War, Mr Williamson was to get no wages during six weeks when Cooper's bottle-works closed down to clean the furnace. So money was tight when Mr Williamson joined the Cameronians. A year later, Mrs Williamson became a conductress on the cable cars for 3 years. The electric cars only came as far as Joppa from Musselburgh. They called the cars "the Sparks".

Mrs Williamson recalls that the Ramsay Tech was originally built as a chocolate factory for a German. But when the First World War broke out, he was interned. During the Second World War, Mrs Williamson worked in the canteen there. It was a munitions works. Soldiers were stationed on top of the building with their guns so that they could see across the Forth.

But I don't think we have to ask Mrs Williamson for memories that recent, or we would obviously have enough for a book.

Isa Brown, October 1980

− PORT0BELL0 SWIMMING CLUB HISTORY
Part 1- SEASIDE ROOTS −

Portobello Swimming Club celebrated its 75th Anniversary this year with a special Annual Swimming Gala. Other city clubs have longer histories but Portobello had some very good swimmers before 1912 and bathing clubs operated all along the beach.

Portobello's first polo internationalist was Lachie McKenzie who scored a goal against England in 1897 − the last time Scotland was to beat England for 88 years! Lachie's last international game was in . 1899 and when the Baths opened in 1902, he was pond attendant He became an instructor in 1912, the year the Club was formed. When Lachie felt a learner wasn't making enough progress, he pitched him into the deep end to sink or swim. There's no record of anyone sinking!

Before 1912, Portobello's good swimmers were members of the Hibernian Club, based at Infirmary Street Baths. They were the best team around and three of their youths formed Portobello ASC in 1912 − William Edward (Ned) Barnie, Walter D Gerrard and Duncan Matthews. Duncan was the first Scottish men's champion in 1911 and became well known as the owner of a china shop on the High Street. Walter Gerrard served many years as an Edinburgh Corporation Councillor (not for Portobello). Ned Barnie, another fine Scottish champion, was a kenspeckle figure who achieved international fame as a three times conqueror of the Channel in 1954. The third local Scottish champion from those days was Eric Thomas (1924).

Three of the club's oldest members took part in a veterans' race in this year's anniversary Gala − J A Fisher, R F G Amos and C Grierson. Jackie Fisher has reason to remember Portobello's first one-mile sea swim for the Sunday Mail Cup which is still flourishing. There was a strong sea running. A rope marked the starting point and the course was laid out around the baths beacon along to Joppa, around the buoy and back via the beacon. With Jackie Fisher ahead, it was between him and Ned Barnie for the finish. Ned, the old hand, let the tide carry him to the beach while Jack fought against it to finish at the starting point. But there was no rule about the finish and Ned was declared the winner. Jackie still chews that one over now and then.

The Ladies' Section was formed in 1922. 1987's Gala welcomed back founder members Ethel Tweedie (nee White), Betty Taylor and Gertie Amos. The Ladies produced many Scottish champions. The first was Margaret Denholm in 1926. In the mid–thirties Eileen Warburton joined the club and won a number of championships from her Portobello base before moving on again. Among the girls of the thirties – like Margaret and Betty Shepherd, Annie Whitson. Jessie Innes (later of Warrender), Marjorie Cresser and Teresa Fusco – there was a host of good swimmers.

Many prominent Portobello people passed through the swimming club. Sir Harry Lauder was a patron and donated a trophy to the Ladies' Section –endowed. There's no record of him giving the Club a donation: maybe he didn't want to belie his stage image.

December/January 1987/88

– SWIMMING HISTORY Part 2 –

Internationalist, Peter Heatly is one of the club's most famous members. Peter's introduction to diving came with the opening of the Open-Air Pool in 1937. That year his grandfather offered the 12-year-old Peter sixpence to go off the 10 metre high dive. Peter thought about it for a long time before he took the first plunge into an incomparable Olympic career.

Peter Heatly won three Commonwealth Games medals on the trot; all three ASA diving titles three years in succession; and many Scottish swimming medals from 50 yards to the half mile. He's been chairman of many top sporting committees including the SASA presidency (one of the best) and a well-deserved OBE.

In 1956 he was the country's best diver but was left out of the Great Britain Olympic Squad by an all-English selection committee. As we'll see later, Portobello had quite an influence on the Scottish committee at the time and got the GB selectors to admit their mistake but not to budge on their decision to leave him out. On his form the results showed he could have won an Olympic highboard medal that year. As it was, his best ever Olympic placing was fifth.

During the 1920s and 1930s when Peter Heatly was growing up Portobello could hold their own with Warrender Club in their heyday.

There was Johnny Heatly (Peter's uncle), Joe Brown, Willie 'Fatty' Phillips, the Tait brothers - Robert, Johnny and Peter (a rugby internationalist too!). Portobello won a number of team races and took pride in their Scottish champions Louis Strachan, Jim Todd and Henry Todd.

The War Years

Elsewhere swimming closed down during the Second World War but Portobello kept going and ran many swimming functions for war charities. The bulk of the work fell to Ned Barnie and the Ladies' Section secretary Marjorie Amos.

In carrying on swimming, the club was unique and had a headstart over other clubs for at least a decade after the war ended. Many swimmers joined Portobello during the war, going back to their own clubs in the end but their influence remained.

Among the ladies, Margaret Carruthers and May Slater were very successful swimmers. Helen Bain (now McLeod-Bain) and her great rival on breaststroke, Isa Veitch, pushed each other to greater efforts. Helen was a wartime member of Portobello. So was Valerie Marrian who became a top diver and swimmer with Warrender.

This was the ladies' heyday of the late 40s and 50s. Lilian Smith, Iris Canning, Lorna Knight, Janice Crease, Elizabeth Goll, Lorraine Mays, Karen Mays, Elma Smith (youngest of three sisters) all won championships and representative honours.

Encouraged by Peter Heatly, Portobello divers were tops - like Louise Barnie, Sheila Currie, Elsie Melville and Geoff Berry.

Service to Swimming Administration

Portobello have always played their part in the Scottish Amateur Swimming Association in and out of the water. Ned Barnie was the seaside club's first SASA president in 1946.

Jimmy Williamson was the longest-serving SASA treasurer (1955-71), president in 1972 and the highly commended swimming administrator of the 1970 Commonwealth Games. Portobello produced two SASA secretaries - Peter Boyd and Jack Snowdon (also polo convener).

The Scottish diving convenership was in the hands of Portobello members from 1949 with Ned Barnie who handed over to James Amos (1950-55) and Peter Heatly (1955-66).

March/April 1988

The "Dirt Track" is built

Sometime in the late twenties a great deal of activity took place in the wasteland between the back greens of Kings Road and the Marine Gardens Ballroom, land which years before had housed an entertainments park. We were entering the age of the Speedway and First Division football.

An embankment gradually took shape round three sides of the ground, a grandstand and clubhouse were built against the side of the ballroom, and a high fence kept out the Kings Road apaches—well, it tried to keep them out. I well remember it didn't keep us out. My mother had made a pair of sack-cloth trousers, which were in at the time. They were set ablaze by something burning in the bing. Had it not been for the dexterity of youth I would have suffered a nasty accident. My eyes still water at the thought.

Eventually all was revealed. The embankments were terraced, the stand was seated, a cinder track was laid around the perimeter of the ground, and a football pitch was laid. An enclosed pen (called the paddock) was brought onto the track through a gate in the safety fence.

Speedway Stars

And now the performers— magnificent men on their two-wheeled machines—names that still bring an excitement: Sprouts Elder, Paddy Deans, local lads Drew McQueen and George McKenzie, all of them heroic figures with the youth of the time. The motor-bikes they rode had famous names which have all but disappeared, Douglas, Rudge, B.S.A., Norton—names that conjure up the unmistakeable smell of Castrol and the almost ear-splitting noise, that disturbed the good residents of Kings Road, straining to hear Carol Gibbons and the Savoy Hotel Orpheans on 2LO.

The Side Shows

For those of us fortunate enough to have windows that overlooked the track, there was a surfeit of Aunts, Uncles and cousins all visiting on dirt-track nights. Great excitement brewed as each supported his favourite. And so with gallons of tea, prepared on the polished iron range, with innumerable sandwiches containing the best John West gobbled in the intervals between races.

As today when Jack Nicklaus, Bjorn Borg, or Keven Keegan appear on T.V., there is a vast upsurge of interest in their sports over the nation, so in those days there were the local side effects. Every street had its own speedway drawn in chalk on the tarmac road, the bikes substituted by steel hoops driven by cleats, manufactured in their dozens by the local blacksmith.

Each street had its team with its own title, and each competitor took the name of his favourite star. Teams from Kings Road, Pipe St., Tower St., and others raced against each other. The trophies were replicas of the real thing. The Gold Helmet was the crown of a bowler hat covered in gold paper which once covered chocolate biscuits.

Cars were distinctly thin on the ground. But there was a profitable side-line for the local youths. They were engaged as programme or chocolate sellers. When you started you were given a brown peaked cap bearing the legend "Cadburys" and a box of one penny bars of nut chocolate, with a commission on sales. The next step was a wooden tray held by a strap around your neck and containing a selection of goodies the cry was "Chocolate two pence, pastilles sixpence a packet".

Regrettably the attraction faded, the crowds disappeared, and speedway closed, to be revived later elsewhere, but not with the same magic.

Football

Concurrently with the speedway Leith Athletic occupied the football pitch, and great was the enthusiasm when they reached the First Division. The famous teams of the day played at Marine Gardens, Celtic and Rangers were at the top then, and I well remember the Celtic goalkeeper John Thomson who was to die so tragically young.

During the years of the speedway there were other attractions mounted. We all boggled at the size of the Heavyweight Champion, Primo Camera, but eventually only the dance hall was left, with its famous dance bands and its four thousand dancers. This too closed on the outbreak of war in 1939.

G. S., May/June 1988

– WHO NEEDED TELEVISION? –

In 1920, my sister and I were brought from a grey Glasgow tenement, where the backcourts were our playground, to a paradise where our playground was real sand. I loved Portobello from the moment I saw it as a child of seven. I loved the house we stayed in. It had a garden with flowers. I loved the sands, ponies - even my bucket and spade - but most of all I think I loved Andre Letta's Pierrot Show.

They performed in a huge marquee at the foot of Wellington Street [now Marlborough Street] and for years the summer really started when the Pierrots opened. Portobello was a duller place when they closed. I often wondered what happened to them in the winter.

Andre Letta was a familiar figure in Portobello. He was a tall, immaculate man, who always wore a flower in his buttonhole. And there was Joy Carol. Rumour had it, she was his sweetheart. Anything else was unthinkable. She was a fascinating person, and some times a little monkey sat on her shoulder. The monkey wore a red coat and she fed it biscuits. She was often in the box office in the afternoons, and if we children saluted smartly and said 'O. H. M. S.!', we were allowed in free to the back row.

Some of the entertainers became well known in theatre music hall. Dave Willis springs to mind, and his son Denny who followed in his footsteps. Denny was just a lad then and played with the boys at their peeries and iron girds.

Donald Peers of Babbling Brook fame, very young and dashing, would walk along the promenade after the show, still in his white tie and tails, with a swirling, scarlet satin-lined cape - eating chips from a newspaper!

Many, many started in the Pierrots in Portobello and the message boys on their bikes whistled their catchy tunes. Who needed television or Top of the Pops?

Sarah Ashcroft, July/August 1989

− FABULOUS FIFTIES −

I was a promenader or, to be more precise, a West End Promenader. I was brought up in a tenement on the sea front in front of the power station, just beside the bathing pool.

All my friends in the stair of my age group had part time jobs either as paperboys or milk boys; very few of the girls were taken on in those days by any of the local shops, don't ask me why. I worked for the grocer cum dairy on the corner of Lee Crescent; I think it was called McWilliams, so my granny got me up at 4.30 every morning. At 5 am I met the Murchie's lorry at the top of Rosebank Lane and looking back on it now I was conned into helping the lorry driver deliver to various dairies along the High Street like "Jessie Melrose" and the one that was opposite Phoenix House, someday will remember the name, before finally delivering to McWilliams. On completing my round it was home for breakfast and then I was free to open up the deckchair store and using a special barrow to take the deckchairs down from Bridge Street to the stance at the slipway at the foot of Rosebank Lane for the lady who hired them out to visitors. The family who owned the deckchair concession was named Clark and lived at the foot of Bath Street. There were four in the family, Benjamin, Luke, Zebediah and Naomi. Luke was an engineer and in his spare time did all the repairs to any broken deckchairs, of which there were quite a few each week. My daily pay was five shillings, two and sixpence for bringing the chairs out in the morning and the same for taking them back each evening. (25 of today's pence per day.) I was a millionaire! I had another little job in the summer holidays, working for Lawrence Cassidy who, as well as a fishmongers business in the High Street, had Sheddan's Restaurant at the foot of Bath Street and the concession for the cafeteria, restaurant, shop and kiosks in the open-air pool. My onerous task was to make sure that the kiosks were stocked with crisps, ice-cream and lemonade, the shop had supplies of Portobello Rock and the restaurants were stocked with fresh fish from the shop and loads of potatoes had been put through the automatic potato peeler. All this took the good part of the morning

Photo courtesy of Mrs Noreen Strachan

Drew Strachan is seated on the right on the deckchair, his grandparents, Hugh and Jenny Greig are on the left and his uncle Tom is in the centre.

but the bonus was that I could go into the pool in the afternoon with my friends after being given my lunch in the cafeteria.

The summers definitely are remembered as being sunnier and it was still exciting to get new sandals or white plimsolls to see you through the season. Great crowds of people came through from the West and hundreds of buses parked in Bridge street, Fishwives

Causeway and Bailleyfield Road. The local kids trawled the beach to collect empty lemonade bottles to exchange for tuppence each at Mr. Doig's shop at the foot of King's Road or at Mrs. Goar's or Mrs. Caskie's. Bottle territories were jealously guarded to stop rival gangs from Pipe Street or Mitchell's Buildings nicking "our bottles". With our ill-gotten gains we could treat ourselves to a poke of buckies or some mussels from the fishwives who had their stalls at the foot of Tower Street (Figgate Street) or Pipe Street or there was Andrew Webber's lorry with all sorts of fruit parked at the foot of Bridge Street.

At the foot of King's Road Mr. Riddle had his pony rides on the beach and if you were lucky enough to get a summer job with him then you had to lead the ponies back to their stables in Ramsay Lane each evening, brush them down and give them their feed. This was a job that the girls went for and competition was so keen that jobs were handed down from sister to sister.

There were all sorts of entertainment on the beach especially during the Glasgow Fair. Various seaside missions set up their stands and had kids singing numbers like Climb, Climb up Sunshine Mountain. The one-man band would perform in his military jacket, tartan trews and the most dismal face I can remember seeing on anybody. There were Punch and Judy shows and, of course, the Salvation Army band. By today's standards it was all very passé but enjoyed by all in the early fifties.

All this was in the summer and when everything closed down in the autumn it was just the milk and paper rounds and back to Gunner Brown's gym club in Towerbank School, the BBs, Scouts or Guides. There were also visits to the County, George or Bungalow cinemas. The Victory was known as the "Bungalow" and was notorious for the attendant walking down the aisles spraying disinfectant over the customers. No wonder it was commonly referred to as the "bug house"!

It all seems so long ago and fairly mundane but I remember my childhood with great affection and would not have wished for anything better.

Drew Strachan, Autumn 2001

– HAPPY DAYS –

Dorothy Addison (formerly Jenkins) who now lives in British Columbia, Canada has sent us some memories of when she lived in Joppa in the late 1940s and 1950s):

"Our family moved to Joppa in 1947. I was ten and my brother John was 13. It was an established community with very few young families. I think there was about only 15 kids ages nine to 12. Joppa then had about 16 shops. Several of them such as the two newsagents, three grocery stores and the dairy, all required delivery boys. None of the girls did this, but we gladly gave the boys a hand with their paper routes. The girls ran messages for neighbours and walked the local dogs, my favourite thing.

I lived at the corner of Joppa Road and Morton Street above Sime and Wilson, the grocers. I left the area when I was a teenager, but there is hardly a day goes by now that I am older, that I do not think of all the happy days of my young life that I enjoyed in Joppa and Portobello, and all the people I knew.

I attended the kinderspiel, a young people's group in Joppa, twice a week and I always wondered where the name kinderspiel came from. The adults in charge organised a concert every year, in Saint Phillip's Church, Joppa. We had such a wonderful time and they were always a great success. I was in quite a few of the shows but unfortunately only have a photograph of one of them. It was called The Country Girl.

At Towerbank School we had a very good netball team which I was a member of. Somebody, I don't know who, took a photograph of us in 1948. I only know the name of the girl holding the ball; she was Rena Taylor and I'm sitting next to her on her left. I can remember the name of the Headmaster. I don't know if that is a good sign or not. His name was Mr Allan.

In my early teens I got a job, along with my friend Dorothy, working at Charlie's Café on the promenade. She was Mr. Frank Cossar's step-daughter and she and I were inseparable. Mr Cossar was a local P.E. teacher. We were reaching 12 years of age and feeling pretty grown up, and desperate to earn some money. Charlie's Cafe was located right next door to where Mr Cossar lived with his family; at the foot of Bath Street, turn left and there was Charlie's.

Dorothy's mother put in a good word for us with Charlie and before we knew it, we were hired for all of our summer school holidays as waitresses and anything else we were able to tackle in his shop. Apart from the kitchen staff we were the only two employees, and we loved it. Charlie was strict but very fair. He put up with no nonsense. He never said much, he only had to look.

The place was busy from morning to night. Our biggest selling specialty was boiling water from our dear old Ascot water heater in the front shop. The line up was non-stop from when we opened, all the way along the counter and out the front door. Every kind of container imaginable was presented to us for a fill up. We charged from sixpence to one shilling and sixpence depending on the size. Anything to get that almighty cup of tea!

In the afternoon, Charlie would disappear to the back of the shop to make his home-made ice cream, and we knew better than to ever disturb him. When that was ready and was brought to the front it was gone in no time. It was so delicious, and the customers knew when to expect it each day.

I went to Canada in 1956 to marry my boyfriend Tom Addison who was from Granton. However, we decided to come back over for the wedding and we got married in St Phillip's in 1957. After our honeymoon in Peebles we returned to Canada. About every second day now I spend time looking at the Edinburgh website run by Peter Stubbs www.edinphoto.org.uk enjoying the photographs and people's recollections of the old days. It would be wonderful to see more photos of Joppa, maybe even a kinderspiel show, and school classes of when I was at Towerbank and Portobello Secondary".

Dorothy Addison (formerly Jenkins), Autumn 2007

PORTOBELLO PEOPLE
– LUCY BETHIA WALFORD: A PORTOBELLO NOVELIST –

Lucy Bethia Colquhoun was born at 11 Brighton Crescent, Portobello [now 11 East Brighton Crescent] on 17th April 1845. Her father was John Colquhoun, second son of the 25th baronet of Colquhoun and was the author of several books.

In June 1869 Lucy married, in St. John's Episcopal Church, Edinburgh, Alfred Saunders Walford, from Cheshire, and it was not until after she had moved to England with her husband that she embarked on her career as a writer, publishing more than fifty books, mainly novels, at the same time as running a home and raising a family.

Nowadays her novels are entirely out of fashion. They can be examined in the National Library of Scotland and the Edinburgh Room of Edinburgh City Library, on George IV Bridge, but I found none on the shelves of the fiction library.

Lucy's Birthplace

The house in which Lucy was born seems to have been built about 1833. In November 1832 a Mrs Ann Cockburn Wauchope, widow of an Edinburgh Writer to the Signet, acquired from John Baxter, an Edinburgh builder, a piece of ground situated on the south side of Brighton Place Crescent. The feu contract required her to have a dwelling house erected, using ashlar from Cullalo or Inverkeithing quarries and the same kind of mason work as the existing houses in the Crescent.

Mr Baxter ensured also that Mrs Wauchope's house would be superior to the others, and in her 'Recollections', published when she was 65, Mrs Walford described it thus: 'All the others were semi-detached, with nice little gardens before and behind; but "The big hoose" stood on its own feet, with a carriage sweep in front, and two large iron gates, one at each end...It was a delightful house of its kind; plain and solid, with two wings....a wild triangle of marsh land fringed with willows was the centre round which Brighton Crescent circled and was frequently the resort of birds of passage.....'

Lucy's father, John Colquhoun, acquired the house in 1843,

together with a piece of ground lying between Brighton Crescent and Rosefield Place, on which he had a stable and coach house erected. He purchased the house fully furnished, probably as it was left by the late Mrs Wauchope. Lucy, remembering it 60 years later, wrote: 'The furniture turned out to be of the best – in the drawing-room it was of rosewood upholstered in pale green satin damask, wonderful for a place like little Portobello'. The china 'proved to be Crown Derby of the best period; Worcester with a glaze that made collectors stare; and Lowestoft'.

Famous Visitors

She remembered also the visitors to the house, particularly the family physician, Dr [later Sir] James Simpson, the discoverer of the anaesthetic qualities of chloroform, her aunt Catherine, writer and philanthropist and daughter of Sir John Sinclair, the author of the first Statistical Account of Scotland [a monument of Catherine Sinclair stands at the foot of North Charlotte Street] and her aunt Julia, the beautiful Countess of Glasgow.

There was also the Newhaven fishwife who called regularly with oysters a shilling the half-hunder and whose bell-like tones of caller oo filled the air with melody.

The family generally spent the summer in the country, at Leny House, Callander when they first occupied the Portobello house, and later at Blackhall Castle, Aberdeenshire. In 1855 Lucy's father bought 6 Eton Terrace, just over the Dean Bridge and the Portobello house was let to the Marquis of Worcester, whose regiment was quartered at Piershill Barracks. In 1860 her father sold 11 Brighton Crescent, together with the stable and coachhouse, to a Mr John Smellie. Later he sold 6 Eton Ter race and bought No. 1 Royal Terrace.

It was when the family were spending a summer at Kames Castle in Bute that Lucy met the kindly old Mr Smith who was the inspiration for her first novel 'Mr Smith, a part of his life', written after she married, and much enjoyed by Queen Victoria, who thereupon asked to have copies of all Mrs Walford's novels as they were published.

In the early years of her career as an author her books were published by Blackwoods and serialised in Blackwood's Magazine, and she frequently called at their place of business in George Street. In her 'Memorials of Victorian London' she wrote that she first met George Eliot in the house of Mr John Blackwood in Edinburgh and that her first novel 'Mr Smith' had 'brought me the friendship of the editor of "Maga". Her correspondence with Blackwoods (preserved in the National Library of Scotland) reveals much of her character and lifestyle.

In 1889 she had a difference of opinion with Blackwoods about issuing cheap editions of her novels and transferred the publication of her literary work to Longmans of London who were less conservative than the Edinburgh firm.

When she died in 1915, she merited an obituary in 'The Times', which suggested that her popularity would probably be short-lived. It ended thus:

'She had a wide and appreciative public, and one of the testimonies to her success which she most appreciated, with regard at any rate to one of her books, was hearing Mr Gladstone, in Chester station, call out of a railway carriage window after a retreating figure: If you want the third volume of "Troublesome Daughters" you will find it on the little table beside my bed".'

Sydney Boyd, August/September 1986

– PORTY'S BANKERS –

Bank of Scotland, Scotland's first bank, made a modest start to doing business in Portobello when it moved into a small shop at 96 High Street in 1958. It joined the Royal Bank of Scotland, the Clydesdale Bank, The National Bank of Scotland, The Commercial Bank of Scotland and The British Linen Bank in the area. The latter bank, The British Linen, was to become inextricably linked to the Bank of Scotland when the two banks merged in 1971. This last event was to have a significant part to play in the Bank of Scotland's connection with the area. Originally occupying two of the four shop units in the building. The British Linen Bank had expanded into the third shop unit in the late 1960s. After the merger, The Bank of Scotland moved the combined business of both branches into the premises at 153 High Street and took over the sole remaining shop unit in the building. The bank re mains there to this day. The two shop units not originally occupied by the bank were at one time a newsagent and a ladies' dress shop called "Sadies", run by a Mrs Geaton.

When the British Linen Bank opened its branch in 1931, newspaper accounts of the day show there was much concern that Portobello had declined from the halcyon days of its heyday as the "Brighton of the North" in Victorian and Edwardian times. We find numerous heart-searching articles in the Edinburgh press, examining why old Portobello had fallen out of fashion. There were repeated calls for the revival of the Portobello pier (built in 1871 and demolished in 1917) to turn Portobello's fortunes. In short, Portobello was at a low period in its history, but it wasn't long before there were strenuous efforts to bounce back. By the mid-1930s work had started on the open air swimming pool, officially opened on Coronation Day in 1937. "The County" cinema in Bath Street (later to become "The George") was a further addition to the area's amenities, opening its doors for business in 1939. An enterprising local entertainer at the time placed an advertisement in the *Edinburgh Evening News*.

> **– Wanted to buy, fleas.**
> **Must be British.**
> **Best prices given.**
> **Apply**
> **Professor Tomlin. Flea Circus,**
> **48 Promenade, Portobello. –**

One wonders whether Professor Tomlin set up his business with a loan from The British Linen Bank.

The branch at Portobello continued to serve the area throughout the War and played its part in raising money for the great effort through the vigorous selling of War Bonds. All able-bodied bankers were, of course, serving their King and Country, and the bank's branches were run by older officials and it was at this time that women became firmly entrenched behind telling counters for the first time.

Today, the branch has changed a lot since the 1930s. Gone are the sombre, dark wood panelled interiors and cumbersome adding machines of yore. Today's bright modern branch offers a variety of computer based services, undreamt of even ten years ago. If the late Mr Alex Harrison ("Harris") Horne JP, the first manager of the branch, could come back today, he would be amazed by the versatility of Home and Office Banking. Even his successor, Mr Douglas Menzies who managed the branch from 1960 to 1980, would not have dreamt that his customers would be able to do their banking transactions sitting in front of their own domestic TV sets at home.

Today the branch is managed by Mr Ken Falconer, who took over in 1980. Conscious of the long serving tradition of Portobello branch managers, he is also very aware that he is presiding over the branch at a time of unprecedented change. Today the bank offers competitive mortgages, a full range of house and contents, car and business insurance services; the bank also pioneered the first high interest cheque account in Britain. Its unique Home and Office Banking Services allow users to check account balances, transfer funds between accounts, check their standing order, and pay bills to any supplier, all at the touch of a button in the customer's own home at any time of the day or night. Business users can opt for the cash management facility which allows them to see funds "in the pipeline" coming through the clearing system. Used in conjunction with the Home and Office Banking high interest investment account, this facility allows the user to maximise on prevailing interest rates.

For details of any of the services mentioned in this article and a free demonstration of the Home and Office Banking Service, call in at the branch and ask to speak to Mr Falconer.

August/September 1986

– JOHN WILLIAMSON'S –
FISH SHOP

The firm of John Williamson, Fishmonger, is an old and interesting one in Portobello. It has been in the same family for several generations.

The present shop at 146 High Street opened in 1901, but the street directory shows a Williamson Jn, Fishmonger, at 72 High Street in 1899, so perhaps the new fishmonger was trying out the trade before moving to permanent or better placed premises. 146 High Street was rented at that time but was bought by the firm in 1926 from John Fusco, Merchant. It was described as 'part of the lands of Figgate at Portobello situated on the north side of the turnpike road leading from Edinburgh to Musselburgh.'

The present owner is Mr James Bonthron. His great -grandfather, also James Bonthron, married Miss Williamson, and thus came into the family business. He was a fisherman and the only survivor of 'The Star of the East' which left Fisherrow Harbour on 29th September 1891 for Lowestoft and was wrecked at the entrance to the harbour there. The fifth generation of Bonthrons, James, the son of the present owner, is now working with his father in the shop. For some years there was a second shop at 330 High Street.

Mr Bonthron started work in the shop when he was 22, having

spent four years at sea. He remembers as a schoolboy in the summer holidays going with his grandfather on his fishing boat to the Isle of Man in pursuit of herring. The equipment at that time was an echo meter and a piece of piano wire which was let down to catch the 'ping' of passing fish; then a ring net with lin. mesh would be put down. Compare this to the sophisti cation of modern electronic equipment.

Mr Bonthron reckons that the blue and white tiles,

Standing outside the shop are, from left to right, Laurence Cassidy, Marion Clark and her brother Archie Bonthron.

depicting fish and fishing scenes, were installed very early on in the life of the shop. He remembers some years ago an old man coming in and saying that he had been the apprentice with the Glasgow firm which had installed them all in one weekend. Now the shop is visited by students from the College of Art who come to admire and record the tiles. The fish sign, carved from a solid block of wood, which hangs above the shop door, is one of the few old shop signs left in Portobello.

Before its recent modernisation the shop used to have a sash window to the street. This was the standard type for a fishmonger's. Mr Bonthron remembers that this was opened first thing in the morning. The fish used to be displayed on large china ashets with a channel to lead off the liquid. When plastic trays had been in use for some time, he was sent down to the cellar below the shop to smash up piles of these beautifully patterned ashets. Buchan pottery jugs and whisky jars also went in this clearing out. The selling of fish has changed greatly over the years. A barrel of herring and salt fish used to stand outside the shop. Mr Bonthron has an old account book of 1947 showing orders of fish sold to a Mrs Learmonth. She would get fish about 11 times in the month for a total of £1.0s.4d. Much of the fish sold then would be ungutted, now about 95% is filleted haddock.

In 1901, when the shop at 146 first opened, John Williamson's neighbours were J Simpson, Boot and Shoemaker at 144 (today Mirson Newsagents), David R Ryder, Grocer, at 140 (today Peter Dominic) and Miss Anderson, Tobacconist at 150 (today Beauty Children's Clothes). His predecessor at 146 was James Simpson, Slater. Less usual trades which seemed to disappear with the century were Lawrence Hislop, Bell-hanger, at 59, and A N Smith, Silk Mercer at 150.

The unusual surname Bonthron is noted first in Scotland at St Andrews in 1617, and Mr Bonthron has been told that it is Huguenot in origin.

Alison Buchanan, March/April 1988

− BRUNSTANE HOUSE'S UNPLEASANT EARL −

This is Brunstane Bridge, popularly known as the "Roman Bridge", that carries the road to Brunstane House over the Brunstane Burn.

Many of us walk past Brunstane House, but few realise that it was once owned by one of Scotland's most powerful earls − John Maitland, who was made Duke of Lauderdale in 1672. He was Secretary of State for Scotland under Charles II and virtually ruled the country for many years .Contemporary reports paint him as a coarse, unattractive man. According to a letter written by Sir Robert Moray to the Duchess of Hamilton, "He must be cannily handled, else a very small provocation will certainly make him quite fly off the hindges."(sic)

In 1692, the Duke appointed Sir William Bruce (the architect who rebuilt the palace of Holyrood-house for Charles II) to draw up plans for massive alterations to Brunstane House. One of the key improvements was a great chamber on the east side of the house, with three windows giving a view over the sea to Fife: windows which still look out over the same view today.

Brunstane Bridge

As part of the improvements Sir William instructed his master mason, Patrick Witherspoon, to build a bridge over the Brunstane Burn – the bridge that still serves as the main approach to Brunstane House today. Known as the 'Roman' bridge, it may stand on the site of an earlier Roman crossing.

The Duke resigned from being the Secretary of State for Scotland in 1680 and settled in Tunbridge Wells. His health deteriorated and he died in 1682. He was buried next to his father in Haddington.

His brother described the funeral, "There were present at the funeral two thousand horses at least, insomuch as they filled the high way for full four miles in length."

A few months before the Duke's death, his wife, the Duchess of Lauderdale became Baroness of Brunstane, but spent most of her later years at Ham House, near Richmond.

Acknowlegements: The above has been extracted from notes kindly supplied by Sydney Boyd, who acknowledges assistance from the Thirlestane Castle Trust for permission to quote from manuscripts in the Lauderdale Muniments.

April 1991

– PORTOBELLO'S 1ST KNIGHT –

In brilliant sunshine, a welcoming party of colourfully garbed members of the Melville Music Hall encouraged passers-by to attend the Scottish Music Hall Society's exhibition, Portobello to the Palace, held in Portobello Town Hall from August 3rd to August 5th. The highlight of the exhibition of Harry Lauder and Scottish Music Hall Memorabilia was the unveiling on Friday the fourth, the 125th

Harry Lauder's grand-niece Greta Lauder-Fraser is flanked on the left by Lord Provost Norman Irons and on the right by entertainer Jimmy Logan as they unveil the memorial plaque.

anniversary of Sir Harry Lauder's birth in Bridge Street, of a plaque in the vestibule of the town hall.

The ceremony was carried out by Greta Lauder Fraser, Grand Niece of Lauder, Jimmy Logan the famous entertainer and Lord Provost Norman Irons, with the aid of a crooked stick one of Sir Harrys props.

The display of a wide range of photographs and posters invoked happy memories for those attending. Eddie Thomson who had a permanent booking at the Palladium for thirty years returned for a second visit and donated his collection of programmes to the Society.

Photographs of Lauder taken with celebrities such as Churchill, Chaplin and Shirley Temple, a collection of various medals conferred on him by various societies worldwide, poster and props vied with copies of birth, marriage and death certificates plus census returns.

Included were samples of caricatures by the late Roy Don whose

23

daughter June Murray, former dancer in the Lex McLean shows loaned them for the exhibition.

Of particular interest to the locals were photographs and advertisements relating to Andre Letta, Tommy Morgan, Dave Willis and others who regularly appeared in Portobello.

Betty Clarkson, of the dancing duo Clarkson and Leslie, whose husband, after their retirement, became Des O'Connor's road manager, exchanged anecdotes with Jimmy Logan, Billy Crockett, June Murray and ex-theatre managers such as Stewart Murray of the King's all of whom expressed their appreciation of the exhibition.

Jimmy Logan taking a break from a gruelling schedule felt that recognition of Lauder in his own hometown was long overdue but was delighted with the plaque. He provided an insight into Lauder's character; concerned about the plight of the disabled after world war one. He raised one million pounds for them. Jimmy's father, Jack Short was one of the beneficiaries, having lost a limb in action and having to be fitted with an artificial leg before resuming his stage career. Ron Marr and the Kyle family came down from Arbroath specially to see the exhibition and Ron recalled Lauder perform there. David Kyle pointed out that it was in Arbroath that Sir Harry made his debut as a singer.

Councillor Maureen Child expressed the majority view when she said, "The organisers are to be congratulated on their hard work which has resulted in a highly successful exhibition featuring something for all those interested in Music Hall and Variety entertainment."

The exhibition was organised by The Scottish Music Hall Society which was formed in 1994 from the Sir Harry Lauder Society and sponsored by The Bank of Scotland. A cash donation was received from The Portobello Commu nity Council and technical expertise was provided by Alex. Hanson, display manager of Scottish Power. Many of the items on display were loaned by the Scottish Theatre Archive housed in Glasgow University Library but a great many were loaned from individual collections. Archie Foley, Chairman of the Society, was extremely pleased with the public's response and thanked all those who helped with the organisa tion and running of the event.

Anne King, Autumn 1995

– MEMORIAL TO SIR HARRY –

Sir Harry Lauder died 50 years ago last month and Portobello Community Council has set up a Committee to raise funds to establish a memorial to honour Scotland's 'first knight of the music hall' who was born on 4 August 1870 in Bridge Street just off Portobello High Street.

Lauder was a theatrical phenomenon, the first truly international superstar, in an age before performers could count on the assistance of jet airliners, satellite communications and electronic wizardry to bring them to the notice of global audiences. His long career took him from the village halls of Lanarkshire, where he had been a coal miner, to the top theatres in London, New York and other great cities all over the world. He made over 20 sell-out tours of North America and numerous visits to Australia and New Zealand covering hundreds of thousands of miles by train and steamship.

Harry Lauder received his knighthood in 1919 for his tireless efforts during World War One. He went to France to entertain the troops and insisted that he would not just do large concerts in bases behind the lines but go as close to the front as possible to boost the morale of those 'in the thick of it.' In a letter, Lauder wrote that after the war he never wanted to see a disabled ex-serviceman having to beg on the streets to make a living and set up the 'Harry Lauder Million Pound Fund' to raise money for the welfare of those injured by the war. He got the money, helped by him undertaking a gruelling tour of America and Canada in 1917 and 1918.

The Memorial Fund Committee has already begun work. A CD of 12 of his classic songs is available now at the excellent price of £10.00 and a commemorative mug bearing one of Lauder's self-caricatures will be on sale soon.

A spokesperson for the Committee said, "Sir Harry Lauder does not just belong to Portobello or even Scotland. He had a worldwide appeal – and still has. At this moment enthusiasts in America are working to raise funds for the memorial. Check out www.sirharrylauder.com and see this for yourself!"

Patricia Ralph, Spring 2000

– COMMUNITY GARDEN PLOT
IN MEMORY OF SIR HARRY –

The project to create a memorial to Harry Lauder in Portobello is now making real progress.

Edinburgh City Council has agreed to the creation of a Community Garden Plot, in memory of Sir Harry, on the piece of land West of Portobello Town Hall and meetings have taken place with officials to fix up the arrangements. After the area is landscaped, visitors will be able to sit on a bench, donated by Portobello Rotary Club, in the shade of a twisted hazel tree (Corylusavellana "Contorta"), whose popular name is the "Harry Lauder Walking Stick Tree", thanks to the generosity of Portobello Garden Centre. A Harry Lauder information board with images and text to illustrate his life is also planned.

The Committee is very grateful to the Rotary Club, the Garden Centre, the other local businesses and individuals for their contributions but a lot more money is required. The fund-raising campaign goes on. Commemorative mugs and CDs are on sale in the library, and if you wish to make a donation, contact Mrs Patricia Ralph at 13 Duddingston Avenue, Edinburgh, EH15 1SJ. Cheques should be made out to the Sir Harry Lauder Memorial Fund.

Queen Mother sends support

A spokesperson for the memorial fund committee said that they had been thrilled and encouraged to receive a letter from Clarence House telling them that, 'Queen Elizabeth was interested to know of the memorial garden Portobello Community Council hope to create in memory of Sir Harry Lauder, who also celebrated his birthday on August 4, and Her Majesty hopes so much that this will come to fruition as it is such a good idea.'

Help from the USA

New England entertainer George Worthley will travel to Portobello in October to honour Sir Harry Lauder and help raise money for his memorial. A Farmington, Maine native, Worthley is one of a few full-time kilted entertainers in the US. Known to the American-Scottish community as "Geordie", he has been a mainstay on the music scene for 30 years and performs throughout the US at folk clubs, festivals and Highland Games. During the last eight years constant companion, and eventual wife, Carol Clark, has joined him. Together they have been bringing a blend of American Scots and UK Scots music to a wide range of audiences, a good deal of it gleaned from the Lauder repertoire of 80 years ago.

Geordie has been booked to appear in St. James's Church Hall on Saturday October 21 at 7.30pm. Local groups will support George and Carol although details are not to hand at the time of writing. Watch for information about tickets. Mark the date and place in your diary!

Patricia Ralph, Autumn 2000

− SIR HARRY LAUDER MEMORIAL GARDEN −

The newly created garden was opened on 4th August, which is the anniversary of Harry Lauder's birth in Bridge Street in 1870. Mr Gregory Lauder-Frost, grandnephew of the world-famous entertainer performed the ceremony and in his speech revealed that the Lauder family link with Portobello was much stronger than generally thought. Mr Lauder-Frost's researches show that Sir Harry's grandfather moved here from Edinburgh and lived at number 2 Ramsay Lane for twenty years with his wife and family, which included Sir Harry's father.

Mr Tom Smith, Chairman of Portobello Community Council, welcomed the guests, which included Mrs Angela Logan, widow of the late Jimmy Logan. Mr Smith pointed out that it was the labours of a large number of people that had helped transform the piece of ground where they were standing into such a lovely little garden and all had to be thanked for their efforts and contributions. He wanted especially to point out, however, the wooden bench that had been provided by Portobello Rotary Club, the twisted hazel tree, gifted and planted by Bill and Ian Thomson of Portobello Garden Centre and the planters donated by Mr James Ralph of Ralph Plastics and acknowledge the work of Mr Scott Thomson of Edinburgh Parks Department. He also read out a letter from the Queen Mother, who shares her birthday with Harry Lauder, expressing her delight at the completion of the garden.

The opening ceremony was followed by a reception in the- Town Hall where local individuals, businesses and organizations that had contributed to the memorial fund were joined by those from further afield including representatives from the Scottish Music Hall Society, which also gave invaluable assistance with the variety show on 1st September as well as donating to the Fund, Edinburgh City Council and the Grand Lodge of Scotland.

Archie Foley, Autumn 2001

− WHERE WAS SIR HARRY BORN? −

Mr Christopher (Chick) Jack emailed *The Reporter* from Edmonton, Alberta when he heard that number 3 Bridge Street, popularly known as Harry Lauder Cottage, was up for sale. He has a particular interest in the property because it was the home of his great grandfather Robert H Jack in the latter half of the 19th century. Then the building was divided into two very small dwellings that were only converted into a single home comparatively recently. Mr Jack asserts: "The commemorative plaque has been placed on the south half of the duplex, which at the time was R H Jack's house...and if it were moved to the right of the existing front door it would be in the proper location representing the correct half of the duplex that Harry was born in".

Where Harry Lauder was actually born has been the subject of local controversy over many years. As shown in the photograph published in 1928 he claimed it was 3 Bridge Street, which was the home of his mother's parents, but this has been hotly disputed over the years by some Portobello citizens who alleged that he had been taken there shortly after birth having been born elsewhere. Bridge Street Lane has been suggested, among others, as a location. Unfortunately no evidence, other than of the anecdotal sort, appears to have ever been produced to support the claims. We know for certain that Lauder's MacLennan grandparents did live in one half of the Bridge Street property also occupied by Mr Jack's forebears. What does exist is his entry in the statutory Register of Births, but even that is not conclusive. It states that Henry [sic] MacLennan Lauder was born on 4th August 1870 in Bridge Street, Portobello but no house number is given. There the matter rests unless and until someone produces irrefutable documentary evidence to settle this issue once and for all.

Spring 2007

– EUROPEAN UNION –

The history society was very pleased to be able to provide Mr Robert Fenley of Sutton Coldfield with copies of old photographs of King's Road and Fishwives Causeway to illustrate his family history. His family was part of the large number of skilled continental, particularly German and Swedish, glassworkers who were recruited to modernize manufacture and improve the quality of the finished product. The following is a shortened version of his story.

"Portobello figures very prominently in the lives of my maternal grandparents. They met and married there, and their first 3 children were born there. But my grandfather's entire family had moved there sometime in 1900 and several other children were born there to his brothers and their wives, each of whom also married in Portobello. For a number of years they all lived in King's Road.

Karl Heinrich Mutzke was an itinerant glassblower and the family had lived in Dresden, Neusattl (Bohemia, now Czech Republic), Italy, St Petersburg and Lyons before coming to Portobello. All 3 of his sons, Oswald Franz (my grandfather), Paul Oskar and Karl Heinrich junior were interned on the Isle of Man in WWI, during which Karl Heinrich senior died in Glasgow. My grandfather and his family moved to London

Louisa with husband and sons after the family was repatriated to Germany. Sons l. to r. are Richard, Walter, Willi, Oswald and Carl.

around 1920 and his brother Paul died there in 1934. His other brother Karl and family moved to Dresden towards the end of WWI and their fifth son was born there in 1919. That son was in the German Army during WWII while his Scottish-born brothers were in the British Army.

Agnes Martha (Nancy) Mutzke was the last direct connection with Portobello -she died there, at 8 King's Road in 1943. But Emma Elizabeth, who had married Bill Crawford in 1928, survived in Scotland until she died in Glasgow in 1975. My Aunt Winnie, born in Portobello in 1908 lives in Eastbourne. As children we were told that our granddad had helped the Portobello Labour Party.

Louisa, wife of Karl Heinrich jnr. with her 4 Scottish born sons, l.to r., Oswald, Richard, Carl & Willi. Taken in Portobello in 1916 when her husband was interned.

I'm in touch with Walter, the one born in Germany in 1919. His brother Richard who lived in Portobello until the family was "repatriated" to Germany visited him in September and they reminisced about those difficult times around WWI.

Richard in particular remembers his older brothers, Willi, Carl, and possibly Oswald, who went to school in Portobello, telling him later about being shouted at as "German pigs" after the start of WWI. The police had to be called out once to smooth things over. But, of course, when they went to Dresden towards the end of the war, they were shouted at as "British pigs"!

A final reflection: my granddad never regarded himself as German. His family clearly originated from German-speaking areas, like Saxony (Dresden), but he and his siblings were born all over Europe and I like to think of them, itinerant glass-blowers, as "European".

Archie Foley, Winter 2001

– SPRINGBOARD TO SUCCESS –

A memorial plaque celebrating the achievements of Sir Peter Heatly has been hung in the Refreshment Room in Portobello Swim Centre. A member of Portobello Amateur Swimming Club (ASC), Sir Peter won many medals as an accomplished diver.

Peter's family came from Leith, where he attended Leith Academy, and he later studied engineering at the University of Edinburgh. When they moved to Portobello Peter made good use of Portobello Baths and taught himself to dive. He dominated the sport for over 20 years. He won the East of Scotland Championship in 1937, the first of many wins, and was Scottish champion from 1946 to 1958. Peter won medals in three consecutive Commonwealth Games: gold for the 10 metre platform and silver in the three metre springboard in Auckland in 1950, gold for the three metre springboard and bronze in the 10 metre platform in Vancouver in 1954, and gold in the 10 metre springboard in Cardiff in 1958, where he was Scotland Team Captain. In the European Games in Turin in 1954 he won bronze for the 10 metre platform. Peter also competed in the Olympic Games in London in 1948 and Helsinki in 1952. He always maintained his connection with Portobello ASC and was made a Life Member in

Photos courtesy of Peter Heatly

1949, and was President from 1952 to 1957.

Following his successful diving career, Peter moved into sports management and, amongst other roles, was Chairman of the Commonwealth Games Council for Scotland, Scottish Sports Council and Commonwealth Games Federation for various periods between 1967 and 1990. He was involved with the planning and design of the Royal Commonwealth Pool, which has an Olympic standard diving pool and is the only venue to have been used for three Commonwealth Games. He attended its opening for the 1970 Games in Edinburgh. A plaque has also been erected there and a meeting room renamed in his honour.

Peter was awarded the CBE in 1971, made a Deputy Lieutenant of the City of Edinburgh in 1984 and knighted in 1990. Sir Peter was inducted into the Scottish Sports Hall of Fame in 2002, the Scottish Swimming Hall of Fame in 2010 and, posthumously, into the International Swimming Hall of Fame in 2016. An internationally recognised athlete and diver, Sir Peter died aged 91 in September 2015.

Margaret Munro, Spring 2017

– LIFE RECORD –

When a friend showed me this photograph of a 78rpm (revolutions per minute) record he had bought it raised two questions. Why did the record have a stamp on it and where had Portobello Gramophone and Music Depot been?

Investigations reveal that the stamps were fixed to records as a form of receipt by the recording companies to show they had paid the mechanical copyright royalties due under various Copyright Acts and General Regulations. This evolved from stamping printed music with the composer's signature to show copyright. These stamps were first introduced in the United Kingdom in July 1912 and had stopped being used by 1939. Records were generally made of shellac between about 1898 and the 1950s, after which vinyl was used. The record, pictured, by Ambrose and his Orchestra was produced about 1930.

Post Office Directories show that Miss M.E.G. Moir ran the depot at 223 Portobello High Street from 1926 until 1938. Previous to this it had been Elsmere Photographic Studio. 223 no longer exists, but was located on Portobello High Street beside Windsor Place Church, where the new flats are now.

Who was Miss Moir? Her home address was given as 25E Abercorn Terrace from 1926 until 1933, with her business address given as her home address from then until 1938. Mary Eliza Graham (M.E.G.) Moir was born on 17th May 1885 at 5 Leith Street Terrace, Edinburgh to Robert Moir, widower, a silver engraver, and Amelia Moir, widow of Alexander Burn, a mercantile clerk. Robert and Amelia were married on 27th December 1880. Robert was 52 years old and Amelia was 34. Her maiden name was Graham. Robert must have been a skilled craftsman, probably making them a middle-class family. This might explain how Meg, as she seems to have been known, could afford to establish such a grandiose-sounding business. It was well stocked. Not only did it sell records and sheet music, but also an assortment of musical instruments, musical novelties and accessories.

It also appears to have been well known across a wider area than Portobello. Evidence of this is given in Tony Smith's biography of footballer Gordon Smith, where it states: "Since moving down to the big

The record bought from Portobello Gramophone and Music Depot with the stamp enlarged in the inserted photo.

city, Gordon would browse all the record stores. In nearby Portobello he would visit Meg Moir's record shop ..."

Meg's death in the Royal Infirmary, from cancer, was recorded on 5th February 1938. She is described on her death certificate as a Music Dealer and single. She seems to have been a successful business woman, with customers coming from a wide area to buy their records and other musical requisites.

Margaret Munro, Winter 2019

– THE DECORATORS OF PORTOBELLO –

Since October 2019, I have been working on the artist residency The Decorators, part of Art Walk Projects Land Mark programme. My residency was based on the former site of the Buchan & Co Thistle Pottery, Bridge Street. As it draws to a close, I reflect here on the work which culminated with the celebratory decorators' tea party on 29th February and the artworks now installed in the kilns and surrounding area.

Photo courtesy of Mairi Fortuna

I focused on women who worked as decorators for the pottery in the late 1960s. Mostly in their teens, the women painted thistles, among other motifs, near the present-day kilns site. Each decorator had her own mark that she would put on the bottom of pottery she decorated. In 1972, Buchan's closed the Portobello site. Some of the women ceased to be decorators at around this point, either through redundancy or moving on to married life. On my site visits, I was struck how the history and work of the decorators were invisible.

Margaret Munro, Portobello Heritage Trust, had interviewed Mairi Fortuna, one of the decorators, in 2017. With Margaret's help, I met Mairi late last summer. Along with sharing her memories, Mairi showed me photographs that captured herself and others at work and play (see page 35). She quickly spread the word about the residency, which led to meetings with three other decorators, and a wealth of memorabilia that included personal photographs, union cards, redundancy notices and, of course, examples of their work. Memories of friendships as well as working conditions were recurring themes that included detailed descriptions of painting thistles. Irene Kozok, who worked at the pottery from 1966 to 1972, told me, "...now, if I close my eyes I can still do it. So, I've never forgotten how to actually paint the thistles on the pots...".

My residency makes visible this social history through the final artworks on location. Interview extracts from three decorators can be heard in the kiln on 7th and 8th March. Chalk logos map out the area of the decorators' workshops nearby, and one of Mairi's photographs is a large photo-banner, also on Bridge Street. A large banner, wrapped around the kiln under restoration, includes the names and signs of all the decorators who have either taken part or been remembered by my interviewees. By working directly with women who were once decorators at Buchan's pottery, the final artworks of my residency aim to make visible their memories of life and work in Portobello. For more information go to www.artwalkporty.co.uk

Nicky Bird, Spring 2020

Editors' note: Mairi Fortuna has given details of the people, all decorators, in her photograph that was taken in 1968. "the girl on the left was then Linda Auchterlonie. The lady in the middle was Kitty Milne (now deceased). The girl on the right was then Karen Mackie. They are both married now."

EDUCATION MATTERS
– PORTOBELLO SCHOOLS –

Photo courtesy Mrs M Meikle

The school at 15 Stanley Street.

A rare copy of the *Portobello Advertiser* for July 22nd, 1885 has been unearthed and among much fascinating material there are lengthy reports on the end of session prize-giving ceremonies at the Burgh School in the then Niddrie Road and Windsor Lodge Academy in Windsor Place. This was a private school for boys on a site now owned by the Post Office. Neither of the Headmasters would have had any fears over league tables according to the glowing accounts of the achievements of both sets of pupils and staff.

The Burgh School was the responsibility of a School Board elected by the voters of Portobello, and its Chairman, Reverend Jamieson, read an extract from the Government Inspector's report: "The large school," it said, "was organized and conducted with superior skill and very marked success." The reporter at the ceremony was particularly struck by the gusto of the singing of the pupils and stated that the "confidence shown by these young people and the way in which they recited and took part in these proceedings was very pleasing."

The Reverend Jamieson was a guest at the ceremony held at

Windsor Lodge Academy where the system he represented was subjected to some criticism from the Reverend Mr Sellar, in charge of proceedings, who declared some objections to School Boards. "They were bound to work for immediate results. They worked under a cast iron system to which all must conform. It was almost impossible to introduce a sys tem which could benefit a large number of boys by bringing them in that mechanical uniformity. In a school like Windsor Lodge the individual character and ability of each pupil could be developed." The headmaster was congratulated for sending up 10 of the 11 boys in the Senior Class to sit the Edinburgh University Local Examinations and for all 10 passing in four of the six subjects. No mention was made of the poor unfortunate not selected for presentation.

In the same paper there was an advertisement for a "Private School for Young Ladies and Kindergarten" at 15 Bath Street and looking through the local paper over the years reveals a number of such establishments, sometimes in unlikely locations. In a January 1901 edition a Miss Hunter (certificated) was advertising that her Ladies School and Kindergarten had reopened on January 8th – "Boarders Received". Rather surprising this was at 9, Dalkeith Street but there was also The Douglas School for Girls at 13 and 15 Brunstane Road "Secondary and Elementary Departments – Pupils prepared for Leaving Certificate and other Examinations." Parental choice in a double measure for the residents of Joppa.

Little information exists on these schools, but we do have a postcard photograph of pupils and staff at the school run by Miss Shiells at 15 Stanley Street at the beginning of the century. This property was bought by Portobello Baptist Church in 1912 and used by them until 1919. This adver tisement was spotted in a June 1934 edition. "Abercorn Lodge School – for Girls and Little Boys – Miss A. Simpson, MA – Prospectus on application." This school at 25 Abercorn Terrace, ran for many years and only closed in about 1950 and some older readers would recall the name of Miss Illingworth and younger ones, Mrs Watson.

Instruction of a more specialised nature could be had at Donald's

Photo courtesy Mrs Joyce Foley

Mrs Watson, staff and pupils at 25 Abercorn Terrace about 1946.

Commercial School in 3 Sandford Gardens where students could tackle Shorthand, Typewriting and Bookkeeping. However, there remains a mystery concerning what may have been the most prestigious education institution in Portobello. Enquiry has failed to solve the meaning of an entry that appears in the Edinburgh and Leith Post Office Directory in the first decade of the century. It gives the occupier and use of 8 Bath Street, Portobello as "Charles Frederick Knight MD – Medical College". This was the mansion, Mount Charles which was eventually demolished to make way for the ScotMid store.

Spring 1998

Editors' note: It didn't take long for the mystery of Dr. Knight and his Medical College to be solved, and the details were revealed in an article in the spring 2007 issue of *The Portobello Reporter*. We included the article in our previous compilation of *Reporter* local history articles. (*Footprints in the Sand*, 2017)

– SCHOOLS IN PORTOBELLO –

The article on private schools in Portobello in the Spring issue of the Reporter brought a response from Mrs. Joyce Campbell who was a decorator in Buchan's Pottery between 1964 and 1972: "In 1906 my mother, Alice Brown, went to the school for girls run by the Misses Douglas at 13-15 Brunstane Road. One of her teachers was a Miss

St Nicholas School about 1936. Malcom Matthews is on the other side of the wolf from Red Riding Hood in the back row. The Queen of Hearts on the right in the centre row is Elizabeth Willins and her brother Bobby is seated on the left in the front row. Other identifications would be welcome.

Niven and she was taught piano by a Miss Blaikie. In fact, she became quite an accomplished pianist. My mother, who died in 1982, was born in a cottage behind the terraced cottages in Joppa Road in 1898.

I, myself attended a dancing school called the St. Nicholas School in 15 Brunstane Road in the 1930s run by Miss Lessels. In one of the displays I played Red Riding Hood and my brother, Stanley Greig - now well known in Jazz circles - was the Wolf. I also went to the Abercorn Lodge School in Abercorn Terrace from 1937 to 1943. This was the school run by Mrs. Illingworth Watson.

My father, Arthur Greig, had a dance orchestra in which he was the drummer and played at dances in the Marine Gardens ballroom. He was a piano tuner to trade and had a shop at Jock's Lodge called The Square Deal which sold pianos and furniture. It was where St. Margaret's House is now. He also sang for many years with the Southern Light Opera company. His father was the David Greig mentioned as the assistant to James Ross in the making of the copy of the Scaliger Railing at Queen's Bay Lodge at the top of South Morton Street. David Greig was a bridge builder and went to Africa where he died of malaria and his wife said she saw his death in a dream."

Autumn 1998

40

PORTOBELLO AT WAR
– MYSTERIOUS KID MURDOCH –

This item was spotted in the sports column of the now defunct *Daily Sketch* for Wednesday, 19th June 1940 while doing research on a project for World War Two: "Kid Murdoch, the well known Scottish boxer, who was reported killed in action and later a prisoner of war, walked into his home at Portobello yesterday, where he saw for the first time his baby boy, born only a few weeks ago. Murdoch boxed with Benny Lynch in an Edinburgh booth in a New Year Carnival. He has been sparring partner to Jake Kilrain."

Enquiries in the files of the *Evening News*, *Daily Record* and *Boxing Monthly* revealed no trace of Kid Murdoch. Brian Donald, boxing historian and author of "The Fight Game in Scotland" put me in touch with a number of old professionals including Joe Aitchison who had been Jake Kilrain's trainer, but nobody could recall a boxer of that name. With every step the mystery deepened. Who was Kid Murdoch? Was he a boxer? Did he live in Portobello and if he did are any of his family still here? At the time of writing the search still goes on, with a few avenues still to explore. Does anyone remember a family named Murdoch who had a particularly happy reunion in June 1940?

April 1991

– WARTIME MEMORIES –

In 1939 I was ten years old and living in Aberdeen because my father, who was a Civil Servant, had been moved there in 1933. In spite of its so-called distance from the war there was general feeling of jitteriness in Aberdeen.

In early summer 1940 my father had been moved back to Edinburgh and my mother was anxious that the family should be reunited with him. It was June of that year when the sirens sounded for real. My older brother Ian, my mother and myself were together in a downstairs room trying to sleep.

There had been the sound of an aeroplane but nothing else, when suddenly I became aware of my mother shutting and bolting the back door. Being inquisitive she had gone out into the garden and suddenly a plane had emerged from behind a cloud. To her horror a 'stick' fell from it; "straight for us" she thought! What we heard was a scream, then another and another, followed by four deafening explosions – in the garden I thought. We were out of bed like greased lightning. We stood there, huddled together in the dark, expecting to be blown to bits at any minute. The bombs were not in the garden but very near the main railway line to the south – a legitimate target.

I think it was the next night the bombers returned. This time the bombs dropped further away from our house but before they departed the bombers flew in low over our houses and strafed them with machine gun fire. Shortly afterwards we returned to Edinburgh and our next encounter with German bombers.

Because our family house in Portobello was let out, we rented a house in Blackhall and spent several nights under the beds. Our Anderson shelter was uninhabitable as it flooded every time there was rain. However, we got back in our family home because the young couple renting it moved away unexpectedly and there were several more incidents during the coming weeks.

A plane was thought to have jettisoned its bomb load on bungalows in Milton Road and a man was killed when a bomb fell near to him just after he had seen his young family into the shelter. He was the local Air-raid Warden and was going on duty.

On 4 August 1940 my parents decided to take us to St. Mark's Episcopal Church in Portobello. Down we went, but as we made to go along the High Street from the foot of Brighton Place barriers and numerous policemen blocked our way. We were told that there were four unexploded bombs in Abercorn Terrace and the Bomb Disposal Unit was up against a serious problem. The bombs had ended up in wet sand and the more the men tried to remove them, the deeper the bombs sank! They, or what's left of them, may still be there.

We did not get to church that week, but I think we went the following week beginning an association with St. Mark's that has lasted to this day.

Sheila M. Love, Spring 2000

– WOMEN'S TIMBER CORPS REMEMBERED –

Mrs Rhoda Paton. 84, of Portobello was invited with other surviving members of the Women's Timber Corps (WTC), to attend the unveiling on 10th October of a memorial statue, in the Queen Elizabeth Forest Park near Aberfoyle, to the women recruited in the 1940s to cut and trim trees for the war effort The statue by Fife based artist Malcolm Robertson, is a female figure in WTC uniform with her right hand raised to her face in what appears to be a salute. Rhoda thought it was a wonderful sculpture, but said she was disappointed that she didn't meet anybody she knew. The WTC in Scotland was set up

Photo by Noel Spencer

Happy Rhoda at statue.

in May 1942, as part of the Women's Land Army and Rhoda Duff, as she then was, joined the girls and women from all walks of life, who were recruited from the age of 17 and posted throughout Scotland. They replaced the men who had gone to war and most of the timber they prepared was used down the mines. Rhoda says: "I thoroughly enjoyed every minute. It was a fantastic life." The Corps was disbanded in August 1946 and has had no official recognition until now and no representative at Armistice Day Parades until recently. In fact, they had become the 'Forgotten Corps'.

Winter 2007

Editors' Note: There is an error in this article. Rhoda's Maiden Name was Paton and her Married Name was Duff.

Further information supplied by one of Rhoda's nieces

Rhoda told me that she volunteered for the Timber Corps when she was in her late teens, 17, I think. (I don't know what her job was then, but she worked at the Bottleworks after she came back to Portobello.) She and a group of other young women were sent for training somewhere in western Edinburgh. She was one of the only two to be selected, which surprised her as she was only 5'.0" tall and of slight build. On her six-week training she learned to identify trees and how to use various saws, etc. She said there were others who worked with the horses pulling the logs down from the hillsides.

She was stationed in Insch, Aberdeenshire. Possibly other places too. Accommodation was in long wooden huts, with a central log burner. The pay was (I think she said) £3.00 a week of which £1.10s. was deducted for board and lodging. She said the food was not good and the cook was awful! She loved her uniform and being in the countryside and always smelling of trees.

They were outside the town where they enjoyed cinema visits. The Catholic women were given bicycles by the local church so that they could attend Masses. When the Protestant women went to church, they had to sit at the back when in uniform.

The Timber Corps women did not get paid if it rained or snowed too hard that they could not leave their lodgings. This meant they did not get paid. However, if the weather lasted for longer than a day, they got some pay.

The Italian solders made little things with their hands that they sold for tiny amounts of money. One soldier was a shoemaker and he saved up enough to buy leather. At the end of the war the Italian soldiers were repatriated, and some decided that they would buy fruit for the Timber Corps women with their savings.

This is all I can recall at the moment. This work was obviously extremely hard, and we all owe a great debt of gratitude to these young women who at last got recognition for their efforts.

– OUR SECRET PAST –

Very few people are aware of a part of Portobello's recent past that has completely disappeared. The Royal Observer Corp (ROC), part of the UK Civil Defence organisation, had an underground monitoring unit on top of the Wisp (OS Map Ref. NT305705), built in the early 1960s in the Cold War period, and officially known as the Portobello ROC Post. The bunker was entered through a metal hatch and shaft, where a 15ft ladder gave access to an underground structure that would have become a temporary home for three ROC observers during any escalating nuclear confrontation.

In the event of a nuclear strike, the observers were trained to evaluate the intensity of the nuclear blast pressure, and measure the level of radioactive fallout. This information would then have been passed to a central control, where it would be mapped, and a judgment made on appropriate emergency planning. Regular training continued until 1991, when the Home Office disbanded the ROC after the collapse of the former Soviet Union ended the perceived threat.

The majority of the 1500 UK ROC bunkers were decommissioned and destroyed after 1991. Cell phone operators purchased some of those remaining, as their strategic positions on high ground were ideal for mobile phone radio masts. However, earlier reorganisation had resulted in the Portobello bunker closing in late1968. Due to opencast mining and landscaping on the Wisp site, no trace of the location now exists.

Further detailed information about the ROC can be found on the Subterranea Britannica Cold War website www.subbrit.org.uk/rsg/roc/history.html

Jim Crockett, Summer 2010

– PLAQUE HONOURS "RAILWAY MAN" –

Eric Lomax, the prisoner of war whose story was told in the film The Railway Man, has been honoured with a commemorative plaque at the house in Bedford Terrace where he was born and lived until

he joined up in 1939, at the start of WW2. He was captured by the Japanese while serving as a signals officer with the Royal Artillery, put to work on the building of the Burma Railway and severely tortured.

The plaque to Mr Lomax, who died aged 93 in 2012, was unveiled at a ceremony on 14th June by Charmaine, his daughter from his first marriage, and local man Nick Stroud who organised the project with the aid of generous sponsorship from ScotRail. The plaque reads: Eric Sutherland Lomax, 1919-2012, "The Railway Man", Lived here 1919-1939.

Charmaine said: "It's a great honour to be here to see my father commemorated in this way, and it was a precious moment for me to see the house where he grew up and the view that he saw from his bedroom window".

Nick Stroud says: "After decades of suffering as a result of the torture, Eric Lomax found it within himself to forgive and befriend Takashi Nagase, the Japanese interpreter who had come to symbolise his torment because, he said: "Sometime the hating has to stop". I thought this remarkable man should be commemorated at the place where he was born and grew up".

The film, starring Colin Firth and Nicole Kidman, was based on Eric Lomax's autobiography The Railway Man, published in 1995.

Autumn 2014

– PORTOBELLO'S FIRST (MILITARY) CASUALTY OF WORLD WAR II –

Photos from left to right; George Miller (l) wearing his Wings, instruction at Montrose and George in civvies.

On 3rd September 1939 Britain declared war on Germany and the very next day, RAF Bomber Command dispatched planes from airfields in south east England to attack installations and ships on Germany's North Sea coast. Among them were 14 Wellington bombers of No. 9 Squadron. Flight Sergeant George Miller from Portobello was on board one of them.

George Miller was born on 21st December 1911, at 15 Joppa Terrace, to William and Margaret Miller who already had four sons and two daughters. The family later moved the short distance to Brunstane Road where George spent his formative years. We do not know what his occupation was between leaving Portobello Senior Secondary School and joining the RAF, but photographs with notes in an album that he kept into his twenties show that he was fond of camping and hiking as a member of the Boy Scouts, up to Rover Scout level, and rowed with the local rowing club. The photographs accompanying this article are from this album, which is now in the safe-keeping of George's nephew Scott Miller, who we thank for lending it to us.

He qualified as a pilot at No. 8 Flying Training School at RAF Montrose in 1936, and the following year was posted to RAF Scampton in Lincolnshire for further training on Handley Page Heyford heavy bombers. These biplanes were being withdrawn from active service,

Heyford bombers flying in formation.

but played a useful role in training. Now a fully-qualified pilot and Flight Sergeant, what was to be his final posting took George to No. 9 Squadron at Honington in Suffolk to fly the recently introduced Vickers designed single-winged Wellington bomber.

The squadron's chosen targets on 4th September were at Brünsbuttel, where the Kiel Canal joins the estuary of the River Elbe. This was a second sortie and was met by concentrated anti-aircraft fire and attacks by German fighters in the air. George Miller and his four fellow crew members died when their plane was shot down, as did all five crew of one other plane that was lost. None of the bodies was recovered.

George Miller is commemorated at the RAF Memorial at Runnymede and his name appears on the carved memorial lectern in Portobello High School.

Archie Foley, Autumn 2019

PORTOBELLO POT-POURRI
– HISTORICAL GEMS FROM JOHN STREET –

Just when I was facing a looming deadline and wondering how to fill this space, I received a telephone call from someone in John Street. Would I be interested in looking at a collection of old papers he had found in a bin bag while having "a bit of a clear-out"? There were one or two old Portobello pieces but while he knew the material was not his he could not remember when he had been given it nor by whom.

Once collected and examined the contents of the bag were revealed to be mainly copies of old British and foreign newspapers and magazines from the months of November and December 1890. Unfortunately, wherever they had been over the years before being put in the bag the papers had not been protected. The bulk were so dirty and torn they had to be thrown out right away and the same fate probably awaits the rest.

Apart from copies of the *Edinburgh Evening News* and *Evening Dispatch*, there is a *Coatbridge Express*, some *Pall Mall Gazettes*, a *Weekly Press* from Philadelphia, a *London Press* from Ontario, a *Times of Morocco* and a number of Scottish temperance journals and others of a political and business nature. In international affairs the results of the American elections – Congressional not Presidential – show quite clearly that the Republicans had been soundly beaten. In Edinburgh, The International Exhibition was closing amid a welter of criticism of financial mismanagement. Portobello Unionists held a meeting in the Old Town Hall (now the Baptist Church) at the end of October at which speakers roundly attacked Mr. Gladstone. There were a few rather tattered envelopes plus an advertising circular addressed to Mr. A. Riach at 20 Abercorn Terrace, probably the original owner of the material. In the 1897 *Edinburgh Directory* Alexander Riach lives at that address. Other material suggests that he was a journalist with the *Evening Dispatch*. If either he or his wife was a supporter of temperance it did not prevent the survival of the wine and spirit catalogue sent by S. Carmichael of 114 High Street that shows bottles of Glenlivet whisky at 42 shillings per dozen.

To balance that, a circular from J. Nesbit of 164 High Street announces the erection of new plant to manufacture aerated waters and the "cylinders for condensing carbonic acid and water have been coated with pure silver".

Photo by Archie Foley.

Pride of place must go to the paper bag that had once contained buns or cakes from Brand's the baker. It may be dirty and crumpled, as seen in the photograph, but to have survived over a hundred years is a miracle.

Archie Foley, Winter 2000

– PUB CRAWLER: THE ORMELIE –

Don't be deterred by the seeming limitless mass of humanity which might confront you as you open the door on a busy night (and most nights are busy at the Ormelie) but take courage and go in, for you will find an interesting hostelry.

First Impression

The immediate impression from the decor suggests that you have been transported in space to the Artisan Bar in Abbeyhill or the Bellevue in Broughton Street, but this is only the result of common ownership. Obviously, bulk buying of flock wallpaper, reproduction light fittings and imitation oak beams makes economic sense!

Service

The speedy and efficient staff will meet your needs from a large stock of spirits and liqueurs. The standard spirit measure is 1/4 Gill, something you rarely come across in city centre bars these days, and a good selection of blended and malt whisky is available. If you are a beer drinker, you are sure to be impressed by the fine pint of McEwan's 80-shilling ale sold here. The Ormelie is a free house so other standard keg beers and lagers are served and their condition is good.

Cleanliness is of a high standard and it's nice to notice that all glasses are dried with a cloth in the old tradition after washing and not placed wet on the shelves. There is a large 'regular' trade (always the sign of a good pub) and they clearly enjoy their pub and the pints served in it.

Social Side

You will see tradesmen, students, labourers, lawyers, policemen, civil servants and teachers which makes for a good social mix and easy-going atmosphere. The pub runs a thriving golf club and its football interest seems to lie out at Gorgie rather than at Easter Road. Dominoes are played in one of the two alcoves off the main bar. The total absence of "piped music" and a selective use of the colour T.V. are other points in its favour.

Its few bad points are the placing of the obligatory fruit machine which tends to obstruct the door to the gent's toilet and the toilet itself seems on the small side for such a busy pub. The Ormelie has an all-day and Sunday licence and the bar is much quieter in the afternoons.

Four star rating – overall this is a pub to be recommended and congratulated for its service and management.

August 1980

– PUB CRAWLER: THE FLYING DUTCHMAN –

This Pubcrawler has been contributed by Danny Blyth who is a Portobello resident and has written for various 'good beer guides in the past.

Given the choice, Wagner's 'Wandering Jew of the Ocean' would certainly have spent his one night off in seven years' sailing over furious seas in the lounge rather than the public bar of this Promenade pub. The lounge is cosy and just the right place for a quiet drink, but the public bar cries out for a facelift

Bare Bar

In the early 1970's a marvellous wood-panelled circular bar and gantry was destroyed to make room for live music and dancing. The venture failed as a music license was not granted. The legacy is a bar lacking a genuine identity. A vacant dartboard and empty trophy cabinet suggest better times in the past. Ageing carpet tiles, fading flock wallpaper, together with continuous television and noisy 'space invader' type machines make for an uncomfortable stay.

Warm people — Cool beer

With that said the 'Dutchman' is quite a warm place in human terms. Pool is played and seems to be heartily enjoyed. The bar service is friendly and there is no shortage of witty local historians supping their beer. The usual Scottish and Newcastle selection of keg beers and lagers are on sale together with a limited selection of spirits. The 'Dutchman' is one of the three pubs in Portobello which stock Worthington's White Shield Ale which is one of the world's finest naturally conditioned bottled beers. It is a credit to the management that this always seems to be in good condition and in regular supply.

Overall, the 'Dutchman' is a bar of some potential and I hope, for the town's sake, that the potential will be realised over the years to come.

Star Rating: Three Stars

(Editor I enjoyed their pint of Younger's Heavy Danny, surprised you didn't mention it.)

October 1980

– PUB CRAWLER: THE GRAPES –

Elderly publicans of Edinburgh will no doubt recall the nickname of 'Vietnam' attributed to a well-known hostelry in Fountainbridge. Nearer to home we have a Bar that will in time earn a nickname along the lines of 'The Belfast Bar This is the Grapes in the High Street'.

Infamy in the retail trade is an exception to the old rule of all publicity being good publicity. On my visit at 8.30 on a mild Thursday (pay night for many) evening there was barely a dozen patrons in the Bar. And almost expectedly, there was some trouble during my 20-minute stay. There was shouting, swearing and the wafting of a walking stick. Prompt, though lenient action by the brave landlady stopped a fracas turning into violence.

I feel that Drybrough's, the owners of this tied house, have much to answer for here. If they were at all serious about bettering this Pub, they would insist upon a policy of stricter management. The custom of those who would elsewhere be unwanted was valued on the night in question, and it seemed that it would take a cavalry sabre and not a walking stick to be wafted in order to merit an ordering out.

The pub itself is as drab inside as its uniform and unimaginative frontage suggests. Bar towels are pinned to the wall at angles to help break the monotony of plastic on plastic. A juke box, a loud television and noisy fruit-machine provide other distractions.

Prices are reasonable for beers and spirits. The beer drinker is offered but a narrow range of three Drybrough's Keg beers and one lager. My pint of Light was very acceptable. Though, like most of Portobello's bars there was no Real Ale.

How the elderly drinkers in Portobello must hanker for a return of the Grapes of yesteryear, when an orderly shop sold Campbell Hope & King's Dark and Crown ales in tranquillity. It is up to Drybroughs alone to stop us from Pipe-dreaming.

Star Rating: zero

Rating League: 1. Ormelie (4 Stars)   2/3 Bluebell; Flying

Dutchman (3 stars) 4. Grapes (Zero) .

(Editor: The new lounge bar of the Flying Dutchman is well worth a visit—pleasant atmosphere and renovation has kept the original features.)

October 1980

– PUB CRAWLER: THE PLOUGH –

This High Street managed house fits neatly into that niche of standardization and dubious taste known as "Welcome Inns".

The pub follows an agrarian theme. The usual countryside trappings of plough buckles, cartwheels, jukebox and coloured spotlighting are all there. It is sad that the theme stops at ornaments and does not include the likes of ploughman's lunches or cask conditioned ale.

My Saturday evening stay was made the more uncomfortable by very loud live folk music. Unnecessary amplifiers made easy listening impossible. A wedged open front door allowed the throbbing of what was a very ordinary sound to spread.

The complete range of S&N keg beers and lagers are all available at fair prices. Spirit range was narrow though and dispensed from a gantry which must at some time have seen service as a luxury bathroom cabinet in some ideal homes exhibition.

I feel it is not unfair to labour the point of the gauche feeling of this appallingly decorated pub, despite the efforts of a keen and friendly manageress and bar staff who run a noticeably clean and tidy shop. Contrary to the Brewers' wishes, I did not feel I was in a pleasant rural setting.

So, I took a seat in the side room at the rear of the bar. Even there, the music bellowed, and the walls were bedecked with props which would be more in keeping with the cellars of the Marquis de Sade rather than a High Street Pub.

Rating – one star – and this only for the manageress who deserves a better shop than this.

Danny Blyth, July 1981

Editors' Note: The Ormelie Bar on Joppa Road still trades under its original name, but on the High Street The Plough has been renamed The Portobello Tap and The Grapes is now named The Portobello Bar. The Flying Dutchman on the Promenade at the foot of Bath Street is rebranded as The Espy.

− VERY EARLY DAYS AT JOPPA −

Norman Hughes is well known as the cheery proprietor of the Rockville House Hotel at Joppa Pans and an active personality in community affairs over the years.

He is also, when he has time, a toiler in the field of local history, and for Norman "local" means just that. For him the concentration on Portobello has been overdone and Joppa has been unjustly neglected. He has set out to redress the balance by collecting as much information as he can on Joppa's past from different sources and putting it all together in what he calls "The Joppa Pans Story".

His investigations have led him into the realm of pre-history and the discovery in 1881 of a Middle Bronze Age cemetery at Magdalen Bridge dating from about 1500 BC.

Workmen removing sand from a site between what was then Magdalen Chemical Works (now Booker's Cash and Carry) and Eastfield Cottages, unearthed a large burial urn filled with human bones from a cremated body.

Further excavation revealed six more of varying sizes, the largest being 16 inches high and 12 inches in diameter at the mouth. In one of the urns a small oval razor was found. In addition to the bones in the urns, two well preserved skeletons − one male and one female − were found about four feet below ground level.

Apart from the razor, a few flint chips and a red deer horn fragment, no other implements were found, but at the time this was described as a remarkable cemetery and the flowerpot shaped and elaborately ornamented urns were regarded as some of the finest unearthed in Scotland.

The urns will be on display when the refurbished National Museum in Queen Street re-opens on St Andrews Day 1998.

(Thanks to Dr Alison Sheridan, Assistant Keeper, Department of Archaeology at the museum for providing the details of this find).

Summer 1991

LET'S SPEND A MILLION!

THE COMMUNIST PLAN FOR BUILDING A BETTER EDINBURGH

By

FRED DOUGLAS

PRICE ONE PENNY

1938

Published by the **EDINBURGH BRANCH** of the **COMMUNIST PARTY OF GREAT BRITAIN**

(For Outline, see Back Cover)

– REVOLUTIONARY PLAN
FOR PORTOBELLO –

There is no shortage of plans, proposals and policies for the possible development of Portobello. A copy of a set of radical ideas contained in a master plan for the whole of Edinburgh put forward in 1938 has been passed to the history society by a well-placed source in local government. It was decided to publish them again now so that they might inform, influence and perhaps inspire those members of steering committees, development groups and feasibility studies currently employed on our behalf.

"New Portobello attractions —
amusement pier and an "Eiffel Tower"

The success of the Portobello Pool as an investment in itself, and as a general and profitable attraction for the resort, justifies pushing forward with new attractions. Particularly is this necessary in view of the many limitations Portobello has to overcome including the bright idea of dumping the Power Station there.

The moon and the mermaids at the end of the pier

The agitation for the Pool was coupled at the time with the idea of an amusements pier. There seems to be no reason to doubt the success of Portobello extending its frontage by pushing outwards to the sea and bringing its visitors still more intimately into communion with the briny. With a bit of luck (and the co-operation of the moon and guitars and the mermaids underneath) the end of the pier might really be romantic sometimes. And it could purvey amusement and entertainment at all times. It would no doubt be a mistake to stick such a structure in the middle of the beach and destroy the sweep of what stretch of sand there is. But the Seafield end could probably stand it.

By elevator to the sky

At the opposite end, namely Joppa, to balance the pier's communion with the sea, there might be communion with the sky, and a bird's eye outlook on the Forth from the top of a Portobello "Eiffel Tower." The construction of Portobello's edition of "Eiffel" or "Blackpool" complete with elevator and observation platform would certainly repay the charge to the visitor in exhilaration of prospect. It would defray the outlay to the city.

Amalgamation with coastal burghs

To develop Edinburgh's potentialities as a seaside resort of wide repute, amalgamation with the capital of all the small coastal burghs down to Port Seton, including Musselburgh and Prestonpans on the way, will have to be seriously considered. This would enable a wide range of attractions to be organised and advertised, including the race meetings, golf links, municipal community camping sites, and so forth. Amalgamation would enable the entire coast to be developed, the roads improved, transport to be unified and fifteen miles of amenity to be created. No centre from Portobello to Port Seton would suffer by it, and if the development were promoted in line with a uniform and generous policy, all would gain."

It would be easy to scoff at these ideas and accuse the author of being naive but at least there was boldness of vision and in the last section he anticipated the benefits of regionalisation although going a lot further than the reformers in 1975 when Lothian Region was created.

Autumn 1997

– THE ORIGINS OF THE
EASTERN GENERAL HOSPITAL –

In 1900 Leith had two Poorhouses, the Northern Poorhouse, now the Northern General Hospital and the South Poorhouse in Great Junction Street. By the end of that year it was obvious that the existing accommodation was inadequate and during 1901 various sites were looked at for a new building to replace the South Poorhouse.

On 17th September 1901 the Council decided to open negotiations to acquire the ground at Seafield owned by Mr Christie Miller. Through his London lawyer, Mr Kekewich, it was agreed that Leith Parish Council would feu 121 acres at Seafield at £40 per acre per annum and entry was set for Whitsunday 1902.

The next obstacle to overcome was how to raise the money. In conjunction with Falkirk Parish Council, facing a similar problem,

Photograph Courtesy of Lothian Health Services Archive, Edinburgh University Library

A large group of dignitaries at the laying of the memorial stone of the new South Leith Poor House in 1906.

Leith Parish Council got a Private Members Bill through Parliament in 1902 to allow Councils to borrow up to seven times the amount raised for relief of the poor in the previous year.

With the financial hurdle cleared the Council invited architects to submit designs into a competition and it was the design of a Leith architect, Mr J.M.Johnston, that was adopted.

The council recommended that Seafield should be built on a plan similar to that of Craiglockhart and the kitchen and laundry arrangements were to be modelled on those at Pilton. On 10th October 1904 the plans were approved by the Dean of Guild and to finance the undertaking the Council borrowed £57,000 at 3.3/8% per annum over 30 years.

There were problems and snags during building. The roads through the site were found to be sloping in the wrong direction, causing flooding in some buildings. Another controversial issue was the wood finish within the Main Hall and Boardroom. Some Councillors objected strongly to its high cost - £583 - but they were overruled on the grounds that "standards should be higher in this part of the building as it was not intended for inmates use but for the councillors themselves".

Among the final details was the erection of a partition in the Dining Room to separate male and female inmates. Both groups could be observed at all times from the high platform on which the staff dined. Male inmates from other poorhouses were drafted in to tidy up the grounds and on the 21 October 1907, everything was ready as the inmates arrived from the now redundant South Poorhouse.

Leith Parish Council continued to look after the poor there until the amalgamation with Edinburgh in 1920. Finally, the City of Edinburgh handed over the buildings to the National Health Service in 1948.

Archie Foley, Summer 1998

– W E HENLEY - LONG JOHN SILVER –

Treasure Island, the amusement arcade on the corner of Bath Street and Straiton Place, is no more, but before we forget it, let me tell you about the Portobello connection with Long John Silver!

The pirate first appeared in a story by Robert Louis Stevenson, 'The Sea Cook', written in 1881 to entertain his 11-year-old stepson while they were on holiday in Braemar. Stevenson's friend, W E Henley, had chronic T B in the bone and had his left leg amputated when only 16 and still at school. When he was 23 the infection recurred in his right foot and amputation was recommended; appalled, he fled to Edinburgh where he was treated by Joseph Lister, leading surgeon at the Royal Infirmary, then in Infirmary Street, who was pioneering the use of antiseptic.

While in hospital, he was visited frequently by Stevenson, and they later collaborated on writing stories and plays. Stevenson confessed to his friend that Henley's 'maimed masterfulness' gave him the germ from which Long John grew. They remained close friends until Stevenson's wife Fanny 'stole' a story by a mutual friend, changed it a little, and published it under her own name. Henley thought this was cheating, and said so; Stevenson could bear no criticism of Fanny and broke with Henley.

But the Portobello connection? When Henley came out of the

Infirmary, remaining leg saved and a long literary career ahead of him, he went to Portobello to convalesce, staying at number 4 Straiton Place. He wrote to a London friend: 'This is the seaside. I am within thirty yards of the Firth of Forth. When there ain't a mist you can see the Fife hills quite plain with the naked eye on the other side'.

The cottage is only a stone's throw from the former 'Treasure Island', which didn't exist in Henley's day, and the haar still comes to haunt us. Next time it rolls in from the sea, go down Bath Street and listen for the sound of a crutch stomping along the Prom, and an echo of a big man cursing like a sea cook!

Alix Gaffney, Autumn 2001

– AN ADDRESS TO
THE PEOPLE OF PORTOBELLO –

This address is of a practical kind and bears on the vital question of the health of Portobello. It is the address of a Portobello resident, and may prove of infinitely more value to Portobello people than a hundred addresses by a world-renowned politician.

Mr F Donnelly, of 16 High Street, Portobello says: - "For the past 20 years I have been a great sufferer from pains across the small of my back and loins that troubled me a good deal, and were at times so severe that they interfered with my business. There were some days when I was so bad that I hardly knew how to hold up at all.

I have also suffered from loss of appetite, bad memory, fitful and broken rest, and I would often rise in the morning more tired than when I went to bed at night.

My kidneys have been in a very bad state and have given me no end of trouble. I have tried everything to get cured, but without success, and as for doctors I think I must have consulted 100 at least in different parts of the country, and none of them could do anything for me.

It was about this time that we began to hear of _____ Backache and Kidney Pills in Portobello and the great good they were doing Portobello people, so I went to Mr Findlay, the chemist, and obtained a box from him and as soon as I began to take them I felt relieved.

I have continued to take the pills, and I am pleased to say I feel quite a different man. I am quite free from pain, my kidneys seem to act naturally and more freely, and I can honestly recommend ———— Backache and Kidney Pills to any who suffer as I did. (Signed) F. Donnelly"

Before similarly afflicted readers write and telephone *The Reporter* for details of this wonderful medicament we have to point that the above is an example of the personal testimony type of advertisement that would have been a common feature in the pages of our predecessor *The Portobello Advertiser*. It is in fact one of a collection of press cuttings dating from the late 1890s to the early 1900s from that journal contained in a small scrapbook given to the local history society by a descendant of two members of the old Portobello Town Council, Baillie Douglas and Cllr. Smart. They are a record of mainly council, golf club, church, and political items concerning Portobello, Musselburgh and Edinburgh, and one can only speculate as to why Mr. Donnelly's kidney problems were considered to be worth preserving for posterity.

Dinners and soirees feature pretty often and included is a report of the speech made by Ex-Provost Wood at the dinner to celebrate the merger of Portobello and Edinburgh in 1896. After recounting the achievements of the Portobello Burgh Council in housing provision, public health and other areas he went on to say, "This was a memorable day in connection with Portobello. It was an epoch-making day...He had himself great expectations. He looked forward to the time when Edinburgh would improve their beautiful beach, which all of them were proud of. That beach, they knew, was second to none in the empire. Bathing could be carried out with the greatest safety and satisfaction. He was satisfied Edinburgh would take advantage of this, and would do all it could to improve the burgh. By doing so it was enhancing its own prosperity." Our aspirations may not have changed a lot over the 100 years or so since the amalgamation but perhaps our expectation level is set a trifle lower.

Archie Foley, Summer 2003

SUBSCRIPTIONS

RECEIVED HERE

FOR BEHOOF OF THE

PORTOBELLO

DESTITUTE & SICK SOCIETY.

An original society Window Notice displayed in local shops in the mid nineteenth century.

One of the oldest, if not the oldest, organisations in Portobello voted itself out of existence at a public meeting on 24th November. The Portobello Benevolent Society was founded in 1830 to look after folk in need in the community before Portobello had become a Burgh. Now after almost 175 years of helping thousands of individuals and families with food, fuel, housing and much else besides, the current Committee decided this year that it was time to bring its good works to an end.

Chairman Bob Aitken explains why the decision was made, "Basically the Society relied on potential beneficiaries being made known to it. This could be done by the local churches or any other body but in recent years fewer and fewer names were being put forward. In 1951, 71 households were given help at Christmas; last year the number was down to 12, all pretty elderly. The Committee doesn't have the resources to seek out deserving cases. Really, we've been overtaken by changes in society."

Some years ago the late David Bayes, a former Secretary of the Society, wrote a short piece about it for the Portobello History Society and the following is a part of his account: "Today, happily, there are excellent relations between the Christian Churches in Portobello, and all major denominations actively participate in the co-operative efforts of the Portobello Council of Churches. There is at least one organisation in Portobello, and probably its oldest, which marks civic and Christian co-operation that has been going on since 1830.

Clearly at that time before Queen Victoria's reign there was poverty in a small and growing community like Portobello, and in particular there existed a clamant need to help the sick and housebound and homeless and to protect the poor against cold, disease and personal misfortunes.

So it was that the Portobello Destitute and Sick Society was established. Its first Secretary was also the first Rector of St Mark's Episcopal Church, Rev G W Drummond, many of whose parishioners were families of workmen in Portobello's pottery, glass and paper industries. Thus started a Society that depended on the voluntary donations of the better-off and from the start, needy and deserving people were identified and assistance given with the purchase of fuel and provisions.

The rather dated title of the Society was changed to the 'Portobello Benevolent Society'. Its function in the Welfare State is quite modest, but within its limited resources, it continues to give help in cases of emergency or pressing need, particularly where other agencies are slow to act and where other resources are inadequate. The geographical area for rendering assistance has always been congruent with the boundaries of the old Burgh of Portobello, but has recently been extended to include the Magdalene area.

Successive office-bearers and committee members coming from all the Portobello churches, continued to co-operate in the unassuming voluntary work. Even today, the Steering Committee comprises lay members of the different Portobello Churches, though not being official representatives of them."

At the final meeting, fittingly held in St Mark's Episcopal Church, it was decided that the Society's funds should be distributed among organisations serving the Portobello community whose aims are broadly similar to those of the Society.

Archie Foley, Winter 2004

– ARCHAEOLOGICAL INVESTIGATION AT LOCAL SITE –

Photograph Courtesy of Scottish private collector.

Recently identified from excavated shards is this superb Portobello blue and white transfer printed bowl, c.1820,

The vacant ground, which was once the site of Portobello's Figure of Eight Railway, has been the subject of an initial program of archaeological evaluation, carried out at the request of John Lawson, the City of Edinburgh Archaeologist. The work was carried out on behalf of the site owners by Graham Brown and the author, working for the Scottish Urban Archaeological Trust (SUAT Ltd). The on-site investigation consisted of excavating and recording four large well-spaced trenches, measuring four by two metres, down to the natural sand.

The site lies at the foot of Bridge Street, adjacent to the Figgate Burn and just to the rear of the two surviving pottery kilns that are the sole remnants of Buchan's large stoneware manufactory, which closed in 1972. It is also adjacent to the now enclosed amusement arcade and the built-over late 18th century harbour.

Although work has just begun on the processing and dating of the large amount of ceramic material recovered from the dig, the preliminary results suggest that the area was still a sandy beach until the sale by John Tough in 1867 of the small short-lived pottery of T. Tough and Co. The new pottery owners, Murray and Buchan, and subsequently Buchan's, expanded enormously both their factory area and production of stoneware. Over the next 30 or so years the area of beach to the north of the enlarged pottery was covered over and built up by huge amounts of broken saggars, stoneware, sanitary ware and general kiln debris, which is now more than three metres deep in places. Certainly the area of the excavation had reached its present level by the beginning of the 19th century.

The preliminary evaluation of the pottery, which has now been washed and marked, is interesting. It shows that in the third quarter of the 19th century Buchan's was also at the forefront of the developing market in sanitary wares, and were producing a fine range of transfer-printed cabinet sinks, etc. as an adjunct to their mainstay of brown stoneware flagons and bottles.

In tandem with the ongoing research on the newly recovered pottery, the author has also begun to catalogue all the Portobello ceramic material presently held both in the National Museums of Scotland and Huntly House Museum. This work is being carried out with the object of making all the previously excavated and salvaged Portobello pottery, much of which dates from the Rathbone period (c1810-1880), available for studying in the form of an illustrated CD which will be distributed free, with the Journal of the Northern Ceramic Society, as the fourth in a series on the potteries along the shores of the Forth.

When carrying out the excavation, a local resident Mr Arthur Jeffery, a former thrower at Buchan's pottery and member of the Portobello History Society, asked if the museum would be interested in a box of pottery shards, which he had recovered from a trench dug by the Water Board at the foot of Pipe Street. The small collection, which dates to the 1820s, is extremely exciting, as it contains fragments of unrecorded transfer prints, and others with rouletted schemes and unusual combinations of variegated banding. Given the importance of this material, I would be extremely grateful to hear from anyone else with shard material or marked pieces from the pre-Buchan era, if only to have them photographed and recorded.

George Haggarty, Spring 2005

– PORTOBELLO'S SIGNAL SUCCESS –

Was Portobello the site of the world's first railway signal box? This possibility is suggested by Cuthbert Hamilton Ellis in his history of the North British Railway in which he describes how: "A quaint thing happened in 1847 when a youth named Robert Skelden [was serving as] pointsman at Hawick Junction (later Portobello East Junction)... with two fixed signals to look after..." [Under the system operating at the time he would have had to go out to each signal several times during his shift to change it as and when necessary. This of course had to be done in all kinds of weather, which Skelden obviously found irksome.] "He found that by rigging some cable with a counterweight improvised from a broken rail-chair he could work both while sitting out of the rain in his box between them." Although Skelden was reported to his superiors the Board of Directors, when they heard of it, thought it a good idea, and the Royal Scottish Society of Arts awarded him a silver medal for his ingenuity.

Not much more than this is known about Robert Skelden. There is only one person of that name recorded in the 1851 census in the whole of Scotland and he lived in Rosebank Square, Portobello. He was an Inspector of Lamps on the railway so could well be the individual mentioned in the book. He was aged 30 in the census, however, so was hardly a youth in 1847 as Hamilton Ellis states. Skelden, his wife and two children disappear from the Scottish statutory records after 1851 and it could be that he went to work in England with the railway company.

(Thanks to Roger Kelly, who alerted me to this piece of Portobello history.)

Archie Foley, Summer 2008

− FROM CLAYPIT TO POPULAR PARK −

The clay pits, in about 1900, at one end of the overhead cable system which carried the clay from the clay beds to Portobello.

Figgate Park was formally opened on 30th April 1938 by Sir Thomas and Lady Mabel Whitson. But where did the Park come from? The land which is now the Park contained large clay deposits which were excavated to supply clay to the Portobello Brickworks and the pottery. The clay pits flooded in 1907. In 1925, The Scotsman reported that Councillors Whitson and Brown asked the Parks Committee to consider the formation of a public park up the valley of the Figgate Burn. The following year Councillor Whitson asked for consideration of that motion to be delayed. Then all went quiet.

Meanwhile Whitson was working hard. He had been an accountant and, as honorary accountant of the 1902-1904 Scottish National Antarctic Expedition led by William S Bruce, has a headland named after him in the South Orkney Isles. By 1931 Lord Provost Whitson had been knighted.

Then the pace picked up. In 1932 Sir Thomas Whitson wrote: "For many years, people passing Portobello station in the train must have been distressed by the ugly outlook across the old clay pits below the railway line".

The Council bought the land from the Abercorn Estates for £2,500 in 1934 and started a major clean-up, which involved filling the clay pits, thought to be 70 feet deep, with 'screened refuse'. Some areas were levelled up with ash, trees were planted and the burn dammed and widened to make ponds and islands: the bill for pumping the water out of the clay pits was £200, landscaping came to £1,850 and fencing topped the lot at £2,000.

On 21st December 1937, *The Scotsman* reported that night skating was in full swing and was to be allowed at Figgate Burn if the ice thickness reached four inches – enough to bear the weight of a crowd. On 30th April 1938 Sir Thomas opened the Figgate Burn Recreation Area, in warm sunshine and mentioned the National Keep Fit Campaign. Councillor Sawers proposed votes of thanks and a bouquet was presented to Lady Whitson by Master Ronald Hay.

Gradually the surrounding area was built up and Duddingston Primary and the current Portobello High School were built alongside; St John's Primary School had been built in 1924.

The Park became a quietly appreciated but almost secret haven for the community, but has not been without threats. In 1948 the Council sought permission from the Abercorn Estates to build "school dining accommodation" in the corner at the end of Hamilton Terrace. For which school and how big is still to be discovered, but it was not done. In 1959 the Council again asked for permission to build in the Park

– on the same site as the abandoned school dining accommodation. As a result six garages appeared, now gone; even today that corner is in mixed ownership. In the last decade or so there have been proposals to build car parking around the Air Training Corps Hut and murmurings about sites for schools.

Today, the Park has a Facebook page, an unending stream of walkers, dogs, bikes, scooters, runners and wild life experts – there are over 140 different plants growing there. All this through the imagination of an accountant and tons of refuse.

Geoff Pearson, Summer 2014

PICTURE STORIES
– PORTOBELLO'S BYGONE DAYS –
horse-drawn tram

Mrs Buchanan of Coillesdene Grove sent us this family photograph of the Portobello to Post Office horse-drawn tram, dated 189 on the back. The tram, owned by Edinburgh and District Tramways Coy. Ltd., has a stairway both back and front, and the lady on the upper deck appears to have been painted in after the after the photo was taken. Joseph McManus, "Tourist Photographer", Dundee, might perhaps have been able to tell us why!

April 1991

Editors' Note: We do not know the year this photograph was taken as the final digit of the date is missing from the caption but we do know that horse trams to and from Joppa were replaced by cable cars on 1st May 1902. In turn these gave way to electric cars using overhead wires on 23rd June 1923. (Thanks to Gavin Booth for this information).

– LIBRARY MARKS CENTENARY –

Portobello Library first opened its doors on October 1, 1897, in what is now the police station, but was then public library, reading room, magistrates court and police station.

It was the second branch library for the city of Edinburgh and was part of the municipal improvements carried out by the new council on the amalgamation of Portobello at a total cost of £54,000.

The library initially had 4000 books, though none for children, and in the first week 1266 were issued. The City Council were then informed that, due to its distance from the Central Library, Portobello needed a larger stock.

To celebrate the Centenary a series of events is planned. No dates are arranged as yet, but these will include talks on the history of Portobello and on tracing a family tree. Details will be posted in the Library.

There will also be a small display of Portobello pottery from September 29 to October 31, courtesy of Huntly House Museum.

On Centenary Day, the staff will dress in Victorian costume and the rules and regulations of that period will be adopted.- So be warned – children's hands will be inspected, toys will be put away and SILENCE will be imposed on all Library users!

If anyone has memories of the old Portobello Library that they would like to share, please contact the Librarian Julia Cormack or any member of staff at Portobello Library, 14 Rosefield Avenue, EH15 1AU (tel. 529 5558).

Autumn 1997

– 20 YEARS CELEBRATED IN STYLE –

Photo by Peter E Ross

Khalid Mir (centre), with group members l-r Archie Foley, Barbara Young, Brenda Molony and Eric Wishart.

Twenty years of publishing of *The Portobello Reporter* were celebrated in style on June 19, when nearly 100 people attended an anniversary party at the Masonic Hall in Figgate Street. They included the founders, the present group, many of those who have contributed over the years, advertisers and community representatives.

A delicious buffet of curries, salads and sweet was enjoyed by everyone, provided through the enormous generosity and community spirit of Mr Khalid Mir, JP, of Porto News, 144 Portobello High Street and the Tan Stand, Brighton Place and President of the Portobello 2000 Hoteliers and Traders Association. He and his family sponsored the event, hiring the hall and bringing over cook Sahid Bais of The Village Curry Out in Glasgow to prepare the meal.

Nostalgia was also on the menu as people swapped news and looked through back copies of *The Reporter*, and it was good to see old friends back in Portobello for the occasion, especially Jack and Marion MacDonald formerly of VIP and now living near Kirriemuir, John Ritchie, Sheila Fletcher (formerly McLellan, of Gemini Boutique), and early group members John and Lesley Danzig.

(Portobello Library holds bound volumes of *The Portobello Reporter* from the first issue. They make fascinating reading).

Brenda Molony, Autumn 2000

– "IT ALWAYS SEEMED TO BE SUNNY" –

Local children in cheerful mood after filming on beach.

THE phrase, "It always seemed to be sunny", or something like it, kept coming up during the interviews for the Portobello History Society memories of Portobello video. So, that's the title to look for when it is launched in the middle of November, but you don't just get a video; with it comes a little book with more photographs and text, adding extra details to what is in the film. The price for all of this will be £12.99 and it is not too early to add it to your Christmas list. The project was made possible by a grant from the East Local Development Committee Community Grants Scheme and was also helped by a donation from Portobello Rotary Club. We would like to thank everyone who helped but here want to pay tribute to the older citizens who contributed their time and memories and the children who really were great to work with – and let's not forget their parents for assistance with the costumes.

Archie Foley, Winter 2004

– HOME AT LAST –

Photo by Margaret Drysdale

Portobello Amenity Society has finally achieved the restoration and re-erection of the three ornamental Coade stone pillars which now form the focal point of the new Community Garden on the Promenade.

These listed structures, dating from the early 19th century, stood in the garden of Argyle House, Hope Lane, for at least 90 years until they were taken into Council storage in 1989, when an extension was built onto the house. They are made of an artificial stone, named after its inventor.

Since then, PAS, Portobello Community council and Portobello History Society have campaigned continually to have them re-erected in Portobello, and thanks to a successful application by PAS to the National Heritage Lottery Fund, this is now almost complete. The Lottery grant provided 80% of the cost, PAS and the Community

Council each contributed £2,400, and the Council generously provided the rest.

Some related community projects, also funded by the Lottery, included the Coade exhibition in the Library window in the summer, and the children's cardboard pillars displayed and judged at the POD Prom Party in August.

The two smaller pillars are identical to the chimneys of Dalmeny House, near South Queensferry, seat of the Earl of Roseberry, family name Primrose. The designs on these are taken from the family crest - a lion holding a primrose. The larger pillar has a hooped design of unknown origin.

How they came to Portobello is a mystery. The local Abercorn Pottery made garden urns in the 1830s, so perhaps they also repaired the Dalmeny chimneys. Some of the pillar sections are of different colours, so perhaps they were 'seconds' that got left behind.

A new crown top to one of the pillars has been skillfully made by PAS member and local potter Alison Robinson, to match the one existing original. Copies of four lion motifs were made and attached by the conservators to two original plain quadrants, to complete a circle. See if you can spot these modern lions.

The entire project has been coordinated by PAS member Celia Butterworth, who well deserves all the credit for its success.

John Stewart, Chair, PAS, Winter 2006

– POTTERY WHEEL COMES FULL CIRCLE –

Photo by Archie Foley

"I have a historic electric wheel from the Portobello pottery. It belonged to a friend who worked there as a young man. He was given the wheel when the factory closed in 1972. If anyone fancies putting it back together and using it, it would be great."

When local potter, Alison Robinson, saw this message on the Scottish Potters Association website announcing that an original Buchan wheel was being offered, free to collect from Stow, she acted immediately: "I thought it would be great to have it working again or it could just be stored in my studio for a Portobello museum, especially while we have former Buchan employees still around to give advice on it. Well, I seized the chance to bring it back. It is some weight!" she said, with a lot of feeling.

Alison's ambition to have it working again in Portobello may take a little while to realise as the wheel is in bits and when it first arrived lacked one crucial part. Even although this has since been found and delivered it is not going to be easy to get the wheel going again, but Alison can call on expert help to fit the bits together and repair the electric motor. One of her pottery students at the Community Centre is a skilled craftsman and electrician who, along with a former pottery worker, has already given the dismembered wheel the once over. He hopes that they can get it back into working order, but it will take some time.

Archie Foley, Spring 2008

– COMPLETION OF KILN REBUILD –

Around 200 people attended the community event, arranged by Portobello Heritage Trust, to celebrate the completion of the pottery kiln rebuild. Professor John Hume, Chair of the Royal Commission on the Ancient and Historical Monuments of Scotland, cut the ribbon. Dayle Salmon and Dave Martin, the bricklayers who completed the work to a very high standard, travelled from England with their wives to join the celebration. In the photograph are, left to right, Dayle Salmon, Professor Hume, Dr Margaret Munro, Chair of the Trust, Professor Ross Buchan, consultant to City of Edinburgh Council, and Dave Martin.

Summer 2014

– PORTOBELLO CO-OP –

Photos by Peter E Ross and Margaret Munro

During recent renovations, readers may have seen the shop name that was revealed at 46 Portobello High Street. As you can see here, it shows a grocery department belonging to Portobello Co-operative Society Limited. A history of the society was published in 1934 giving details of its development to that date.

According to the history, in 1846 the Co-operative Movement was in its infancy and there were no overall guidelines to help draw up a constitution for the proposed Portobello society. This, however, only served to 'emphasise the courage and initiative shown by the pioneers of our society'. Several local men acquired premises at 77 Portobello High Street, at the junction with Adelphi Place. Initially these men ran the society, but it grew so rapidly that a full-time salesman, who later become manager, was appointed.

In 1872, premises were purchased at what became number 42. These were converted into a large store with bake-house below and manager's house above. Expansion on this site continued until it was decided to build new premises which opened in 1882. The business now consisted of a grocery, bakery, butchery and drapery departments. These became the central premises of the society, which now owned all the land between Bridge Street and Pipe Street and down to Bridge Street Lane. Further building was undertaken and the tenements above the shops were added. If you stop and look up at the turret on the building at the top of Pipe Street, you can see several of the symbols of co-operation, including the handshake of friendship and the beehive of industry. There is also a stone plaque on the front of the building with the intertwined society initials carved into it.

Growth continued. Land was leased in Windsor Place to graze cattle and sheep. The society ran a fleet of motor and horse vans which serviced the surrounding area. New branches were opened at 201 Portobello High Street, King's Road, Niddrie Mill and Joppa. A new bakery was built at the foot of Tower Street (now Figgate Street) with plans to open a hall and tearoom.

When I moved here in 1973, I did my weekly shopping in the Co-op at 201, now Costcutter. Soon large supermarkets seemed to be the way forward and smaller co-ops struggled. During the late 1970s and 1980s, St Cuthbert's Co-operative Society took these over, including Portobello. Scotmid was created, local branches were closed and a supermarket was built in Bath Street.

Margaret Munro, Summer 2019

– REBUILD ON HOLD –

Photo: Andrew Mylne

Portobello Heritage Trust has been informed by a council official that the rebuild of the 1906 kiln has been put on hold due to the "budgetary financial restrictions" currently in place at the council. A contractor has been selected, but has been asked to hold the price until the new financial year, when the rebuild will be reviewed. Both bottle kilns are Scheduled Ancient Monuments and are the last two surviving large-scale commercial pottery kilns in Scotland. As such, the council, under the direction of Historic Environment Scotland, is obliged to maintain and preserve them.

Similarly, the reinstatement of the municipal clock onto the Baptist Church building may also be placed on hold due to "budgetary constraints".

Spring 2020

The Portobello Reporter was 40 years old in June 2020 and Archie Foley and Peter E Ross decided to celebrate this landmark by putting together another selection of local history articles culled from its pages. Archie is a former member of *The Reporter* group and curates a local history Facebook page. Peter designs the paper and is a current member of the group.

ISBN 978-0-9934028-2-1

9 780993 402821